pasta

pasta

MURDOCH BOOKS

contents

pasta pronto

It was famous film director Federico Fellini who said 'Life is a combination of magic and pasta'. He obviously knew what he was talking about. It is not only the Italians who are passionate about their pasta — it has become a staple in kitchens all around the world.

It is difficult to go wrong with pasta. Even the simplest pasta recipe, such as butter and shavings of parmesan melted over some fresh tagliatelle, can be exquisite. All you have to remember is that pasta should be cooked until '*al dente*' which in Italian literally means 'to the tooth'.

Many people assume that fresh pasta is better than dried but it depends on the sauce. If you are using a rich sauce made from cream, butter and cheese then fresh pasta is ideal. Dried pasta is the better alternative when you have a tomato-based sauce. Of course, these rules aren't set in stone. Part of the appeal of pasta is it's versatility and variety, so be adventurous and experiment with different types, shapes and flavours.

There are a few simple guidelines that should be followed though, to ensure the best results are achieved. Short pastas are best with meat and tomato sauces, as the tubes catch the sauce in their holes. Filled and flavoured pasta should be paired with simple sauces. Long thin pasta go well with simple sauces, and the flatter types work well with creamy sauces that stick to their lengths. Curly shapes suit thick, chunky sauces which get caught in their shape. *Buon appetito*!

short

Penne all'arrabbiata

2 tablespoons olive oil
2 large garlic cloves, thinly sliced
1–2 dried chillies
800 g (1 lb 12 oz) tinned tomatoes
400 g (14 oz) penne
1 basil sprig, torn into pieces

Cook the pasta in a large saucepan of boiling salted water until *al dente*. Drain well and return to the pan to keep warm.

Meanwhile, heat the olive oil in a saucepan over low heat. Add the garlic and chillies and cook until the garlic is light golden brown. Turn the chillies over during cooking so both sides get a chance to infuse in the oil. Add the tomatoes and season with salt. Cook gently, breaking up the tomatoes with a wooden spoon, for 20–30 minutes, or until the sauce is rich and thick.

Add the basil to the sauce and toss with the pasta. Season to taste.

SERVES 4

Artichoke risoni

30 g (1 oz) butter
1 tablespoon olive oil
2 fennel bulbs, sliced
340 g (12 oz) marinated artichoke hearts,
    drained and chopped
300 ml (10½ fl oz) pouring (whipping) cream
1 tablespoon dijon mustard
3 tablespoons dry white wine
50 g (1¾ oz/½ cup) grated parmesan cheese
375 g (13 oz) risoni
130 g (4¾ oz) shredded English spinach
toasted Italian bread, to serve

Heat the butter and oil in a frying pan over medium heat. Add the fennel and cook for 20 minutes, or until caramelised. Add the artichoke and cook for a further 5–10 minutes.

Stir in the cream, mustard, white wine and parmesan and bring to the boil. Reduce the heat and simmer for 5 minutes.

Meanwhile, cook the pasta in a large saucepan of boiling salted water until *al dente*. Drain well and return to the pan to keep warm.

Add the pasta and spinach to the sauce and cook until the spinach has wilted. Serve with toasted Italian bread.

SERVES 4

Orecchiette with baby spinach and pumpkin

750 g (1 lb 10 oz) pumpkin
(winter squash), such as
butternut or jap
2 tablespoons parmesan-
infused olive oil (see Notes)
16 unpeeled garlic cloves
250 g (9 oz) cherry tomatoes,
halved

500 g (1 lb 2 oz) orecchiette
200 g (7 oz) baby English
spinach leaves
200 g (7 oz) marinated Persian
feta cheese (see Notes)
3 tablespoons sherry vinegar
2 tablespoons walnut oil

Preheat the oven to 200°C (400°F/Gas 6). Cut the pumpkin into large cubes, put
in a roasting tin and drizzle with the parmesan-infused oil. Roast for 30 minutes,
then add the garlic. Arrange the tomatoes on a baking tray. Place all the vegetables
in the oven and roast for 10–15 minutes, or until cooked. Don't overcook
the tomatoes.

Meanwhile, cook the pasta in a large saucepan of boiling salted water until
al dente. Drain well and return to the pan to keep warm.

Toss together the pasta, tomatoes, pumpkin, garlic and spinach in a large bowl.
Drain the feta, reserving 3 tablespoons of marinade. Whisk the reserved marinade,
sherry vinegar and walnut oil together. Pour over the pasta and sprinkle with
pieces of the feta.

SERVES 4

NOTES: Parmesan-infused olive oil is available at gourmet food stores and
adds depth of flavour. Persian feta is softer and creamier than other feta and is
marinated in oil, herbs and garlic.

Creamy pesto
chicken penne

1 tablespoon oil
40 g (1½ oz) butter
400 g (14 oz) boneless, skinless
  chicken breast
170 g (6 oz) thin asparagus, cut
  into 4 cm (1½ inch) lengths
3 spring onions (scallions),
  chopped
4 garlic cloves, crushed
300 g (10½ oz) sour cream

125 ml (4 fl oz/½ cup) pouring
  (whipping) cream
185 ml (6 fl oz/¾ cup) chicken
  stock
100 g (3½ oz/1 cup) grated
  parmesan cheese
30 g (1 oz) finely chopped basil
2 tablespoons toasted pine nuts
400 g (14 oz) penne
basil leaves, to garnish

Heat the oil and half the butter in a large frying pan over high heat. Add the chicken and cook for 5 minutes on each side, or until just cooked. Remove, cover and cool, then cut into 1 cm (½ inch) slices.

Add the asparagus and spring onion to the pan and cook for 2 minutes, or until the asparagus is just tender. Remove. Wipe the pan with paper towels.

Reduce the heat to medium and add the remaining butter and the garlic. Cook for 2 minutes, or until golden brown. Add the sour cream, cream and stock, and simmer for 10 minutes or until reduced slightly. Add the parmesan and basil and stir for 2 minutes, or until the cheese has melted. Return the chicken and asparagus to the pan. Add the pine nuts and cook for 2 minutes to heat through. Season.

Meanwhile, cook the pasta in a large saucepan of boiling salted water until *al dente*. Drain well and return to the pan to keep warm. Combine the sauce and the pasta. Garnish with basil leaves.

SERVES 4

Pasta gnocchi with grilled capsicum

6 large red capsicums (peppers), halved
400 g (14 oz) pasta gnocchi (see Note)
2 tablespoons olive oil
1 onion, thinly sliced
3 garlic cloves, finely chopped
2 tablespoons shredded basil leaves
whole basil leaves, to garnish
shaved parmesan cheese, to serve

Cut the capsicums into large flattish pieces. Cook, skin side up, under a hot grill (broiler) until the skin blackens and blisters. Cool in a plastic bag, then peel the skin.

Cook the pasta in a large saucepan of boiling salted water until al dente. Drain well and return to the pan to keep warm.

Meanwhile, heat the oil in a large frying pan, add the onion and garlic and cook over medium heat for 5 minutes, or until soft. Slice 1 capsicum into thin strips and add to the onion mixture.

Chop the remaining capsicum, then purée in a food processor until smooth. Add to the onion mixture and cook over low heat for 5 minutes, or until warm.

Toss together the sauce and pasta. Season, then stir in the shredded basil. Garnish with the basil leaves and serve with the parmesan.

SERVES 4–6

NOTE: Pasta gnocchi is similar in shape to potato gnocchi. If unavailable, use conchiglie or orecchiette.

Penne with mushroom and herb sauce

2 tablespoons olive oil
500 g (1 lb 2 oz) button mushrooms, sliced
2 garlic cloves, crushed
2 teaspoons chopped marjoram
125 ml (4 fl oz/½ cup) dry white wine
4 tablespoons pouring (whipping) cream
375 g (13 oz) penne rigate
1 tablespoon lemon juice
1 teaspoon finely grated lemon zest
2 tablespoons chopped flat-leaf (Italian) parsley
50 g (1¾ oz/½ cup) grated parmesan cheese

Heat the oil in a large heavy-based frying pan over high heat. Add the mushrooms and cook for 3 minutes, stirring constantly to prevent the mushrooms from burning. Add the garlic and marjoram and cook for a further 2 minutes.

Add the white wine to the pan, reduce the heat and simmer for 5 minutes or until nearly all the liquid has evaporated. Stir in the cream and cook over low heat for 5 minutes, or until the sauce has thickened.

Meanwhile, cook the pasta in a large saucepan of boiling salted water until *al dente*. Drain well and return to the pan to keep warm.

Add the lemon juice, zest, parsley and half the parmesan to the sauce. Season to taste. Toss the pasta through the sauce and sprinkle with the remaining parmesan.

SERVES 4

Casarecce with roasted tomatoes, rocket and goat's cheese

16 roma (plum) tomatoes
1 handful basil leaves, torn
400 g (14 oz) casarecce
4 tablespoons olive oil
2 garlic cloves, finely sliced
2 tablespoons lemon juice
120 g (4¼ oz) rocket (arugula),
 roughly chopped

2 tablespoons chopped flat-leaf
 (Italian) parsley
35 g (1¼ oz/⅓ cup) grated
 parmesan cheese
100 g (3½ oz) goat's cheese,
 crumbled

Preheat the oven to 160°C (315°F/Gas 2–3). Score a cross in the base of the tomatoes. Put in a heatproof bowl, and cover with boiling water. Leave for about 30 seconds, then transfer to cold water and peel the skin away from the cross. Cut in half and place cut-side up on a wire rack over a baking tray. Season liberally and scatter with the basil leaves. Put the tray in the oven and bake for 3 hours.

Meanwhile, cook the pasta in a large saucepan of boiling salted water until *al dente*. Drain well and return to the pan to keep warm.

Heat the olive oil and garlic over low–medium heat until it just begins to sizzle. Remove immediately and add to the pasta with the tomatoes, lemon juice, rocket, parsley and parmesan. Stir gently to combine, allowing the heat from the pasta to wilt the rocket. Serve topped with the crumbled goat's cheese.

SERVES 4

Macaroni cheese with pancetta

390 g (13¾ oz/2½ cups) macaroni
75 g (2½ oz) pancetta, diced
500 ml (17 fl oz/2 cups) pouring (whipping) cream
125 g (4½ oz/1 cup) grated cheddar cheese
260 g (9¼ oz/2 cups) grated gruyère cheese
100 g (3½ oz/1 cup) grated parmesan cheese
1 garlic clove, crushed
2 teaspoons dijon mustard
½ teaspoon paprika
2 tablespoons snipped chives, plus extra to garnish

Cook the pasta in a large saucepan of boiling salted water until *al dente*. Drain well and return to the pan to keep warm.

Meanwhile, cook the pancetta in a large saucepan over high heat, stirring, for 4 minutes or until well browned and slightly crisp. Drain on paper towel. Reduce the heat to medium, stir in the cream and simmer. Add the cheeses, garlic, mustard and paprika. Stir for 5 minutes, or until the cheeses have melted and the sauce has thickened. Season.

Add the pasta and pancetta and stir for 1 minute, or until heated through. Stir in the chives, garnish with the extra chives and serve.

SERVES 4

Penne with pork and fennel sausages

6 Italian pork and fennel
   sausages (about 550 g/
   1 lb 4 oz)
1 tablespoon olive oil
1 small red onion, finely chopped
2–3 garlic cloves, crushed
½ teaspoon chilli flakes
300 g (10½ oz) field or button
   mushrooms, thinly sliced

800 g (1 lb 12 oz) tinned
   chopped tomatoes
1 tablespoon finely chopped
   thyme
500 g (1 lb 2 oz) penne rigate
grated parmesan cheese,
   to serve

Split the sausages open, remove and crumble the filling and discard the skins.

Heat the oil in a large saucepan over medium–high heat. Cook the onion for
3–4 minutes, or until fragrant and transparent. Add the garlic, chilli flakes,
mushrooms and crumbled sausage meat. Cook over high heat, stirring gently to
mash the sausage meat, for 4–5 minutes, or until the meat is evenly browned.
Continue to cook, stirring once or twice, for about 10 minutes.

Stir in the tomato and thyme, then bring the sauce to the boil. Cover and cook
over medium–low heat for 20 minutes, stirring occasionally to make sure the
sauce doesn't stick to the bottom of the pan.

Meanwhile, cook the pasta in a large saucepan of boiling salted water until
al dente . Drain well and return to the pan to keep warm.

Add the pasta to the sauce and stir to combine. Serve with the parmesan.

SERVES 4

Orecchiette
with broccoli

750 g (1 lb 10 oz) broccoli, cut into florets
450 g (1 lb) orecchiette
3 tablespoons extra virgin olive oil
½ teaspoon dried chilli flakes
30 g (1 oz/⅓ cup) grated pecorino or parmesan cheese

Blanch the broccoli in a large saucepan of boiling salted water for 5 minutes, or until just tender. Remove with a slotted spoon, drain well and return the water to the boil.

Cook the pasta in the boiling water until *al dente*. Drain well and return to the pan to keep warm.

Meanwhile, heat the oil in a heavy-based frying pan over medium heat. Add the chilli flakes and broccoli and cook, stirring, for 5 minutes, or until the broccoli is well coated and beginning to break apart. Season. Add to the pasta, stir through the cheese and serve.

SERVES 6

Eggplant, ricotta and pasta pots

200 g (7 oz) straight macaroni
125 ml (4 fl oz/½ cup) light
  olive oil
1 large eggplant (aubergine),
  cut lengthways into 1 cm
  (½ inch) slices
1 small onion, finely chopped
2 garlic cloves, crushed

400 g (14 oz) tinned chopped
  tomatoes
400 g (14 oz) ricotta cheese
80 g (2¾ oz/1 cup) coarsely
  grated parmesan cheese
15 g (½ oz) shredded basil,
  plus extra to garnish

Preheat the oven to 180°C (350°F/ Gas 4). Cook the pasta in a large saucepan of boiling salted water until *al dente*. Drain well and return to the pan to keep warm.

Heat 2 tablespoons of the oil in a non-stick frying pan over medium heat. Cook the eggplant in three batches for 2–3 minutes on each side, or until golden, adding 2 tablespoons of oil with each batch. Remove and drain well on paper towel.

Add the onion and garlic to the pan and cook over medium heat for 2–3 minutes, or until just golden. Add the tomato and cook for 5 minutes, or until most of the liquid has evaporated. Season.

Combine the ricotta, parmesan, basil and pasta in a bowl. Line the base and sides of four 375 ml (13 fl oz/1½ cup) ramekins with eggplant, trimming any overhanging pieces. Top with half the pasta mix, pressing down firmly. Spoon over the tomato sauce, then cover with the remaining pasta mixture. Bake for 10–15 minutes, or until heated through. Stand for 5 minutes, then run a knife around the ramekin to loosen. Invert onto plates and garnish with basil.

SERVES 4

Casarecce with pumpkin and feta

1 kg (2 lb 4 oz) butternut pumpkin (squash),
   peeled and cut into 2 cm (¾ inch) chunks
1 red onion, thinly sliced
8 garlic cloves, unpeeled
1 tablespoon rosemary leaves
4 tablespoons olive oil
400 g (14 oz) casarecce
200 g (7 oz) marinated feta cheese, crumbled
2 tablespoons grated parmesan cheese
2 tablespoons finely chopped flat-leaf (Italian) parsley

Preheat the oven to 200°C (400°F/Gas 6). Put the pumpkin, onion, garlic and rosemary in a roasting tin. Drizzle with 1 tablespoon of the oil and season. Rub the oil over all the vegetables and herbs until well coated. Roast for 30 minutes, or until the pumpkin is soft and starting to caramelise.

Cook the pasta in a large saucepan of boiling salted water until *al dente*. Drain well and return to the pan to keep warm.

Squeeze the roasted garlic out of its skin and place it in a bowl with the remaining oil. Mash with a fork.

Add the garlic oil to the pasta, then stir through the remaining ingredients. Toss to combine. Season to taste.

SERVES 4

Penne carbonara

400 g (14 oz) penne
1 tablespoon olive oil
200 g (7 oz) piece pancetta or bacon, cut into
    long thin strips
6 egg yolks
185 ml (6 fl oz/¾ cup) pouring (whipping) cream
75 g (2½ oz/¾ cup) grated parmesan cheese

Cook the pasta in a large saucepan of boiling salted water until *al dente*. Drain well and return to the pan to keep warm.

Meanwhile, heat the oil in a frying pan over high heat. Cook the pancetta for 6 minutes, or until crisp and golden. Remove with a slotted spoon and drain on paper towel.

Beat the egg yolks, cream and parmesan together in a bowl and season well.

Return the pasta to its saucepan and pour the egg mixture over the pasta, tossing gently. Add the pancetta and cook over very low heat for 30–60 seconds, or until the sauce thickens and coats the pasta. Season and serve immediately.

SERVES 4–6

NOTE: Be careful not to cook the pasta over high heat once you have added the egg mixture, or the sauce risks being scrambled by the heat.

Orecchiette with cauliflower, bacon and pecorino

750 g (1 lb 10 oz) cauliflower, cut into florets
500 g (1 lb 2 oz) orecchiette (see Note)
125 ml (4 fl oz/½ cup) olive oil, plus extra, to drizzle
150 g (5½ oz) bacon, diced
2 garlic cloves, finely chopped

80 g (2¾ oz/½ cup) pine nuts, toasted
45 g (1½ oz/½ cup) grated pecorino cheese
15 g (½ oz) chopped flat-leaf (Italian) parsley
60 g (2¼ oz/¾ cup) fresh breadcrumbs, toasted

Bring a large saucepan of salted water to the boil and cook the cauliflower for 5–6 minutes, or until tender. Drain.

Cook the pasta in a large saucepan of boiling salted water until *al dente*. Drain well and return to the pan to keep warm.

Heat the oil in a frying pan over medium heat. Cook the bacon for 4–5 minutes, or until just crisp. Add the garlic and cook for 1 minute, or until just golden. Add the cauliflower and toss well.

Add the pasta to the pan with the pine nuts, pecorino cheese, parsley and 40 g (1½ oz/½ cup) of the breadcrumbs and stir to combine. Season, sprinkle with the remaining breadcrumbs and drizzle with a little extra oil.

SERVES 4

NOTE: Orecchiette means 'little ears' in Italian. If unavailable, use conchiglie or cavatelli.

Zucchini pasta bake

200 g (7 oz) risoni
40 g (1½ oz) butter
4 spring onions (scallions), thinly sliced
400 g (14 oz) zucchini (courgettes), grated
4 eggs
125 ml (4 fl oz/½ cup) pouring (whipping) cream
100 g (3½ oz) ricotta cheese (see Note)
100 g (3½ oz/⅔ cup) grated mozzarella cheese
75 g (2½ oz/¾ cup) grated parmesan cheese

Preheat the oven to 180°C (350°F/ Gas 4). Cook the pasta in a large saucepan of boiling salted water until *al dente*. Drain well and return to the pan to keep warm.

Meanwhile, heat the butter in a frying pan over medium heat. Add the spring onion and cook for 1 minute. Add the zucchini and cook for a further 4 minutes, or until soft. Allow to cool slightly.

Combine the eggs, cream, ricotta, mozzarella, pasta and half of the parmesan. Stir in the zucchini mixture. Season well. Spoon into four 500 ml (17 fl oz/2 cup) greased ovenproof dishes. Sprinkle with the remaining parmesan and bake for 25–30 minutes, or until firm and golden.

SERVES 4

NOTE: With such simple flavours, it is important to use good-quality fresh ricotta from the delicatessen or the deli section of your local supermarket.

Penne with tomato and basil sauce

500 g (1 lb 2 oz) penne rigate
4 tablespoons extra virgin olive oil
4 garlic cloves, crushed
4 anchovy fillets, finely chopped
2 small red chillies, seeded and finely chopped
6 large vine-ripened tomatoes, peeled, seeded and diced
4 tablespoons white wine
1 tablespoon tomato paste (concentrated purée)
2 teaspoons sugar
2 tablespoons finely chopped flat-leaf (Italian) parsley
3 tablespoons shredded basil
grated parmesan cheese, to serve (optional)

Cook the pasta in a large saucepan of boiling salted water until *al dente*. Drain well and return to the pan to keep warm.

Meanwhile, heat the oil in a frying pan over medium heat. Cook the garlic for 30 seconds. Stir in the anchovy and chilli and cook for a further 30 seconds. Increase the heat to high, add the tomato and cook for 2 minutes. Add the wine, tomato paste and sugar and simmer, covered, for 10 minutes, or until thickened.

Toss the tomato sauce and herbs through the pasta. Season and serve with grated parmesan, if desired.

SERVES 4

Conchiglie rigate
with spring vegetables

500 g (1 lb 2 oz) conchiglie rigate
310 g (11 oz/2 cups) frozen peas
310 g (11 oz/2 cups) frozen
  broad (fava) beans, blanched
  and peeled
4 tablespoons olive oil
6 spring onions (scallions), cut
  into 3 cm (1¼ inch) pieces
2 garlic cloves, finely chopped

250 ml (9 fl oz/1 cup) vegetable
  or chicken stock
12 thin fresh asparagus spears,
  cut into 5 cm (2 inch) lengths
½ teaspoon finely grated
  lemon zest
3 tablespoons lemon juice
shaved parmesan cheese,
  to garnish

Cook the pasta in a large saucepan of boiling salted water until *al dente*. Drain well and return to the pan to keep warm.

Meanwhile, put the peas in a saucepan of boiling water and cook over high heat for 1–2 minutes, or until tender. Remove with a slotted spoon and plunge into cold water. Add the broad beans to the saucepan of boiling water and cook for 1–2 minutes, then drain and plunge into cold water. Remove and slip the skins off.

Heat 2 tablespoons of the oil in a frying pan over medium heat. Add the spring onion and garlic and cook for 2 minutes, or until softened. Pour in the stock and cook for 5 minutes, or until slightly reduced. Add the asparagus and cook for 3–4 minutes, or until bright green and just tender. Stir in the peas and broad beans and cook for 2–3 minutes, or until heated through.

Toss the remaining oil through the pasta, then add the vegetables, lemon zest and lemon juice. Season and toss together well. Serve topped with shaved parmesan.

SERVES 4

Orecchiette with mushrooms, pancetta and smoked mozzarella

400 g (14 oz) orecchiette
2 tablespoons olive oil
150 g (5½ oz) sliced pancetta, cut into short thin strips
200 g (7 oz) button mushrooms, sliced
2 leeks, sliced
250 ml (9 fl oz/1 cup) pouring (whipping) cream
200 g (7 oz) smoked mozzarella (mozzarella affumicata),
    cut into 1 cm (½ inch) cubes
8 basil leaves, torn

Cook the pasta in a large saucepan of boiling salted water until *al dente*. Drain well and return to the pan to keep warm.

Meanwhile, heat the oil in a large frying pan over medium–high heat. Add the pancetta, mushrooms and leek and sauté for 5 minutes. Stir in the cream and season with pepper. Simmer over low heat for 5 minutes. Stir in the pasta. Add the mozzarella and basil and toss.

SERVES 4

Penne with roasted tomato and pesto

140 ml (4¾ fl oz) olive oil
500 g (1 lb 2 oz) cherry tomatoes
5 garlic cloves, unpeeled
400 g (14 oz) penne rigate
90 g (3¼ oz/⅓ cup) pesto
3 tablespoons balsamic vinegar
basil leaves, to garnish

Preheat the oven to 180°C (350°F/ Gas 4). Put 2 tablespoons of oil in a roasting dish and place in the oven for 5 minutes. Add the tomatoes and garlic to the dish, season well and toss until the tomatoes are well coated. Return to the oven and roast for 30 minutes.

Meanwhile, cook the pasta in a large saucepan of boiling salted water until *al dente*. Drain well and return to the pan to keep warm.

Squeeze the flesh from the roasted garlic cloves into a bowl. Add the remaining olive oil, the pesto, vinegar and 3 tablespoons of the tomato cooking juices. Season and toss to combine. Add to the pasta and mix well. Gently stir in the cherry tomatoes, then scatter with basil.

SERVES 4

Farfalle with spinach and bacon

400 g (14 oz) farfalle
2 tablespoons extra virgin olive oil
250 g (9 oz) bacon, chopped
1 red onion, finely chopped
250 g (9 oz) baby English spinach leaves, stalks trimmed
1–2 tablespoons sweet chilli sauce (optional)
35 g (1¼ oz/¼ cup) crumbled goat's cheese

Cook the pasta in a large saucepan of boiling salted water until *al dente*. Drain well and return to the pan to keep warm.

Meanwhile, heat the oil in a frying pan over medium heat. Add the bacon and cook for 3 minutes, or until golden. Add the onion and cook for a further 4 minutes, or until softened. Toss the spinach leaves through the onion and bacon mixture for 30 seconds, or until just wilted.

Add the bacon and spinach mixture to the pasta, then stir in the sweet chilli sauce, if using. Season and toss well. Scatter with the crumbled goat's cheese to serve.

SERVES 4

Penne with tomato and onion jam and olives

3 tablespoons olive oil
4 red onions, sliced
1 tablespoon soft brown sugar
2 tablespoons balsamic vinegar
800 g (1 lb 12 oz) tinned chopped tomatoes
500 g (1 lb 2 oz) penne rigate
150 g (5½ oz) small pitted black olives
75 g (2½ oz/¾ cup) grated parmesan cheese

Heat the oil in a non-stick frying pan over medium heat. Add the onion and sugar and cook for 25–30 minutes, or until caramelised.

Stir in the vinegar, bring to the boil and cook for 5 minutes. Add the tomatoes, return to the boil, then reduce the heat to medium–low and simmer for about 25 minutes, or until the tomatoes are reduced and jam-like.

Meanwhile, cook the pasta in a large saucepan of boiling salted water until *al dente*. Drain well and return to the pan to keep warm. Add the tomato mixture and olives and stir to combine. Season and top with the grated parmesan.

SERVES 4

Porcini mushroom and walnut penne

20 g (¾ oz) porcini mushrooms
400 g (14 oz) penne rigate
2 tablespoons olive oil
1 onion, finely chopped
2 garlic cloves, crushed
24 button mushrooms, sliced
3 thyme sprigs
90 g (3¼ oz) walnuts
2 tablespoons sour cream
grated parmesan cheese, to serve

Put the porcini in a bowl with just enough boiling water to cover and leave to soak for 30 minutes. If they soak up all the water quickly, add a little more.

Cook the pasta in a large saucepan of boiling salted water until *al dente*. Drain well and return to the pan to keep warm.

Heat the oil in a deep frying pan over medium heat. Add the onion and garlic and cook until translucent but not browned. Add the porcini and any soaking liquid, mushrooms and thyme. The mushrooms will give off liquid as they cook so continue cooking until the liquid is soaked up again.

In a separate frying pan, fry the walnuts over medium heat without any oil until they start to brown and smell toasted. Allow to cool slightly, then roughly chop and add to the mushroom mixture. Toss with the pasta, stir through the sour cream and season. Serve with the parmesan.

SERVES 4

filled

Conchiglione stuffed with roast pumpkin and ricotta

1 kg (2 lb 4 oz) butternut pumpkin (squash),
  cut into large wedges
olive oil, to drizzle
10 unpeeled garlic cloves
500 g (1 lb 2 oz) ricotta cheese
20 g (¾ oz) finely shredded basil
750 ml (26 fl oz/3 cups) ready-made tomato pasta sauce
125 ml (4 fl oz/½ cup) dry white wine
56 conchiglione or 32 giant conchiglione
100 g (3½ oz/1 cup) grated parmesan cheese

Preheat the oven to 200°C (400°F/ Gas 6). Place the pumpkin in a baking dish, drizzle with olive oil and season. Bake for 30 minutes, then add the garlic and bake for 15 minutes or until tender. Allow to cool slightly, then peel and mash the pumpkin and garlic. Mix with the ricotta and half the basil and season to taste.

Put the pasta sauce and wine in a saucepan and bring to the boil over medium heat. Reduce the heat and simmer for 10 minutes, or until slightly thickened.

Meanwhile, cook the pasta in a large saucepan of boiling salted water until *al dente*. Drain well. Lay out on a tea towel (dish towel) to dry, then fill with the pumpkin mixture. Spread any remaining filling in a large ovenproof dish, top with the shells and pour on the sauce. Sprinkle with parmesan and the remaining basil and bake for about 15–20 minutes (or 30 minutes for the giant shells).

SERVES 6

Spinach and ricotta ravioli

1 tablespoon olive oil	2 egg yolks, beaten
1 red onion, finely chopped	2 tablespoons grated
1 garlic clove, crushed	parmesan cheese
200 g (7 oz) baby English	freshly grated nutmeg
spinach leaves, coarsely	48 won ton wrappers
chopped	40 g (1½ oz) butter
250 g (9 oz/1 cup) ricotta cheese	2 tablespoons sage leaves

Heat the oil in a frying pan over low heat. Add the onion and garlic and fry for 2–3 minutes, or until the onion is soft and translucent. Add the spinach and stir until wilted.

Stir the spinach mixture into the ricotta, along with the egg yolk, parmesan and some nutmeg. Season.

Brush a little water around the edge of a won ton wrapper and put 1 teaspoon of filling in the centre. Fold the wrapper over to make a half moon shape and press the edges firmly together. Lay out the ravioli on a tea towel (dish towel) and repeat with the remaining wrappers.

Cook the pasta in a large saucepan of boiling salted water until *al dente*. Remove with a slotted spoon and drain well.

Melt the butter in a small saucepan over medium heat. Add the sage and cook for 1–2 minutes, or until the butter browns slightly. Pour the butter and sage mixture over the pasta and serve.

SERVES 4

Tortellini boscaiola

30 g (1 oz) butter
4 bacon slices, chopped
2 garlic cloves, crushed
1 small leek, thinly sliced
300 g (10½ oz) Swiss brown or button mushrooms, sliced
3 tablespoons dry white wine
375 ml (13 fl oz/1½ cups) pouring (whipping) cream
1 teaspoon chopped thyme
500 g (1 lb 2 oz) fresh veal tortellini
50 g (1¾ oz/½ cup) grated parmesan cheese
1 tablespoon chopped flat-leaf (Italian) parsley

Melt the butter in a large frying pan over medium heat. Add the bacon and cook for 5 minutes, or until crisp. Add the garlic and leek, and cook for 2 minutes. Add the mushrooms and cook for 8 minutes, or until softened. Add the wine, cream and thyme and bring to the boil. Reduce the heat and simmer for 10 minutes, or until the sauce has thickened.

Meanwhile, cook the pasta in a large saucepan of boiling salted water until *al dente*. Drain well and return to the pan to keep warm.

Add the parmesan to the sauce and stir over low heat until melted. Season. Combine the sauce with the pasta and parsley.

SERVES 4–6

Veal agnolotti with alfredo sauce

625 g (1 lb 6 oz) veal agnolotti
90 g (3¼ oz) butter
150 g (5½ oz/1½ cups) grated parmesan cheese
300 ml (10½ fl oz) pouring (whipping) cream
2 tablespoons chopped marjoram (see Note)

Cook the pasta in a large saucepan of boiling salted water until *al dente*. Drain well and return to the pan to keep warm.

Meanwhile, melt the butter in a saucepan over low heat. Add the parmesan and cream and bring to the boil. Reduce the heat and simmer, stirring constantly, for 2 minutes, or until the sauce has thickened slightly. Stir in the marjoram and season. Toss the sauce through the pasta.

SERVES 4–6

NOTE: Any fresh herb such as parsley, thyme, chervil or dill can be used instead of marjoram.

Ham and cheese pasta bake

1½ tablespoons olive oil
1 onion, finely chopped
300 g (10½ oz) leg ham, sliced 3 mm (⅛ inch) thick and
    cut into 5 cm (2 inch) lengths
600 ml (21 fl oz) pouring (whipping) cream
300 g (10½ oz) cooked fresh peas or frozen peas, thawed
375 g (13 oz) conchiglione
3 tablespoons roughly chopped basil
250 g (9 oz) grated mature cheddar cheese

Preheat the oven to 200°C (400°F/Gas 6). Lightly grease a 2.5 litre (87 fl oz/10 cup) ovenproof ceramic dish.

Heat 1 tablespoon of the oil in a frying pan over medium heat. Cook the onion, stirring frequently, for 5 minutes or until soft. Add the remaining oil, then the ham and cook, stirring, for 1 minute. Pour the cream into the pan, bring to the boil, then reduce the heat and simmer for 6 minutes. Add the peas and cook for a further 2–4 minutes, or until the mixture has thickened slightly. Season.

Meanwhile, cook the pasta in a large saucepan of boiling salted water until *al dente*. Drain well and return to the pan to keep warm.

Add the sauce to the pasta, then stir in the basil and three-quarters of the cheese. Season. Add the mixture to the prepared dish, sprinkle on the remaining cheese and bake for 20 minutes, or until the top is golden brown.

SERVES 4

Veal tortellini with creamy mushroom sauce

500 g (1 lb 2 oz) veal tortellini
3 tablespoons olive oil
600 g (1 lb 5 oz) Swiss brown mushrooms, thinly sliced
2 garlic cloves, crushed
125 ml (4 fl oz/½ cup) dry white wine
300 ml (10½ fl oz) thick (double/heavy) cream
pinch ground nutmeg
3 tablespoons finely chopped flat-leaf (Italian) parsley
30 g (1 oz) grated parmesan cheese

Cook the pasta in a large saucepan of boiling salted water until *al dente*. Drain well and return to the pan to keep warm.

Meanwhile, heat the oil in a frying pan over medium heat. Add the mushrooms and cook, stirring occasionally, for 5 minutes, or until softened. Add the garlic and cook for 1 minute. Stir in the wine and cook for 5 minutes, or until the liquid has reduced by half.

Combine the cream, nutmeg and parsley. Add to the sauce and cook for 3–5 minutes, or until the sauce thickens slightly. Season. Divide the tortellini among four serving plates and spoon over the mushroom sauce. Sprinkle with parmesan cheese.

SERVES 4

Beetroot ravioli with sage burnt butter sauce

340 g (12 oz) tinned baby
   beetroot (beets)
40 g (1½ oz) grated parmesan
   cheese
250 g (9 oz) fresh ricotta cheese
4 fresh lasagne sheets

fine cornmeal, for sprinkling
200 g (7 oz) butter, chopped
5 g (⅛ oz) sage leaves, torn
2 garlic cloves, crushed
shaved parmesan cheese,
   to serve

Drain the beetroot, then grate it into a bowl. Add the parmesan and ricotta and mix well. Lay a sheet of pasta on a flat surface and place evenly spaced tablespoons of the ricotta mixture on the pasta to give 12 mounds — four across and three down. Flatten the mounds of filling slightly. Lightly brush the edges of the pasta sheet and around each pile of filling with water.

Place a second sheet of pasta over the top and press around each mound to seal and enclose the filling. Using a pasta wheel or sharp knife, cut the pasta into 12 ravioli. Lay them out on a lined baking tray that has been sprinkled with cornmeal. Repeat with the remaining filling and lasagne sheets to make 24 ravioli. Gently remove any air bubbles after cutting so that they are completely sealed.

Cook the pasta in a large saucepan of boiling salted water until *al dente*. Drain well, then divide among four serving plates.

Meanwhile, melt the butter in a saucepan until golden brown. Remove from the heat, stir in the sage and garlic and spoon over the ravioli. Sprinkle with shaved parmesan and season.

SERVES 4

Roasted vegetable cannelloni

60 g (2¼ oz) butter
1 large leek, cut into 1 cm
  (½ inch) pieces
200 g (7 oz) chargrilled
  eggplant (aubergine) in oil
200 g (7 oz) chargrilled orange
  sweet potato in oil

125 g (4½ oz/1 cup) grated
  cheddar cheese
40 g (1½ oz/⅓ cup) plain
  (all-purpose) flour
1 litre (35 fl oz/4 cups) milk
6 fresh lasagne sheets

Preheat the oven to 200°C (400°F/Gas 6). Lightly grease a 28 x 18 x 5 cm (11¼ x 7 x 2 inch) ceramic dish. Melt 20 g (¾ oz) of the butter in a saucepan, add the leek and stir over medium heat for 8 minutes, or until soft. Chop the eggplant and sweet potato into 1 cm (½ inch) pieces and place in a bowl. Mix in the leek and 40 g (1 ½ oz/⅓ cup) of the cheddar.

Melt the remaining butter in a saucepan over medium heat. Stir in the flour and cook for 1 minute, or until foaming. Remove from the heat and gradually stir in the milk. Return to the heat and stir until the sauce boils and thickens. Reduce the heat and simmer for 2 minutes. Season. Stir 375 ml (13 fl oz/1½ cups) of the sauce into the vegetable mixture, adding extra if necessary to bind it together.

Cut the lasagne sheets in half widthways to make two smaller rectangles. Spoon the vegetable mixture along the centre of one sheet and roll up. Repeat to make 12 tubes in total. Place the tubes, seam-side-down, in the dish and spoon the remaining sauce over the top until they are covered. Sprinkle with the remaining cheese and bake for about 20 minutes, or until the top is golden.

SERVES 4

Ravioli with roasted red capsicum sauce

6 red capsicums (peppers)
625 g (1 lb 6 oz) ravioli
2 tablespoons olive oil
3 garlic cloves, crushed
2 leeks, thinly sliced
1 tablespoon chopped oregano
2 teaspoons soft brown sugar
250 ml (9 fl oz/1 cup) vegetable or chicken stock

Cut the capsicum into large flattish pieces and remove the membrane and seeds. Cook, skin side up, under a hot grill (broiler) until the skin blackens and blisters. Cool in a plastic bag, then peel the skin.

Cook the pasta in a large saucepan of boiling salted water until *al dente*. Drain well and return to the pan to keep warm.

Meanwhile, heat the olive oil in a frying pan over medium heat. Cook the garlic and leek for 3–4 minutes, or until softened. Add the oregano and brown sugar and stir for 1 minute.

Place the capsicum and leek mixture in a food processor or blender, season and process until combined. Add the stock and process until smooth. Gently toss the sauce through the pasta over low heat until warmed through.

SERVES 4

Veal tortellini with baked pumpkin and basil butter

1 kg (2 lb 4 oz) jap pumpkin (winter squash),
   cut into 2 cm (¾ inch) cubes
600 g (1 lb 5 oz) veal tortellini
100 g (3½ oz) butter
3 garlic cloves, crushed
80 g (2¾ oz/½ cup) pine nuts
45 g (1½ oz) shredded basil
200 g (7 oz) feta cheese, crumbled

Preheat the oven to 220°C (425°F/Gas 7). Line a baking tray with baking paper. Place the pumpkin on the prepared tray and season well. Bake for 30 minutes, or until tender.

Meanwhile, cook the pasta in a large saucepan of boiling salted water until *al dente*. Drain well and return to the pan to keep warm.

Heat the butter in a small frying pan over medium heat until foaming. Add the garlic and pine nuts and cook for 3–5 minutes, or until the nuts are starting to turn golden. Remove from the heat and add the basil. Toss the basil butter, pumpkin and feta through the pasta.

SERVES 4

Roasted chunky ratatouille cannelloni

1 eggplant (aubergine)	350 g (12 oz) cannelloni tubes
2 zucchini (courgettes)	3 tablespoons shredded basil
1 large red capsicum (pepper)	300 g (10½ oz) ricotta cheese
1 large green capsicum (pepper)	100 g (3½ oz) feta cheese
3–4 ripe roma (plum) tomatoes	1 egg, lightly beaten
12 unpeeled garlic cloves	50 g (1¾ oz) pecorino pepato
3 tablespoons olive oil	cheese, grated
300 ml (10½ fl oz) tomato	
passata (puréed tomatoes)	

Preheat the oven to 200°C (400°F/ Gas 6). Cut the eggplant, zucchini, capsicums and tomatoes into 2 cm (¾ inch) cubes and place in a baking dish with the garlic. Drizzle with the oil and toss to coat. Bake for 1 hour 30 minutes, or until the vegetables are tender and the tomatoes slightly mushy. Peel and lightly mash the garlic cloves.

Pour the passata over the base of a large ovenproof dish. Spoon the ratatouille into the cannelloni tubes and arrange in the dish.

Combine the basil, ricotta, feta and egg in a bowl. Season well and spoon over the cannelloni. Sprinkle with the pecorino and bake for 30 minutes, or until the cannelloni is soft.

SERVES 6–8

Salmon and ricotta-stuffed conchiglione

200 g (7 oz) conchiglione
(about 32)
425 g (15 oz) tinned red
salmon, drained, bones
removed and flaked
500 g (1 lb 2 oz) fresh ricotta
cheese
1 tablespoon chopped flat-leaf
(Italian) parsley

3 tablespoons chopped chives
1½ celery sticks, finely chopped
90 g (3¼ oz/¾ cup) grated
cheddar cheese
185 ml (6 fl oz/¾ cup) pouring
(whipping) cream
25 g (1 oz/¼ cup) grated
parmesan cheese

Preheat the oven to 180°C (350°F/Gas 4). Cook the pasta in a large saucepan of boiling salted water until *al dente*. Drain well and return to the pan to keep warm.

Combine the salmon, ricotta, parsley, chives, celery and cheddar in a large bowl and season.

Put 2 teaspoons of filling in each shell. Place the filled shells into a 3 litre (105 fl oz/12 cup) ceramic baking dish.

Pour over the cream and sprinkle with the parmesan. Cover with foil and bake for 20 minutes, then remove the foil and bake for a further 15 minutes, or until golden brown. Spoon the cream sauce over the shells and serve.

SERVES 4

Sweet potato ravioli

500 g (1 lb 2 oz) orange sweet potato, chopped
2 teaspoons lemon juice
190 g (6¾ oz) butter
50 g (1¾ oz/½ cup) grated parmesan cheese
1 tablespoon chopped chives
1 egg, lightly beaten
250 g (9 oz) packet won ton wrappers
2 tablespoons sage, torn
2 tablespoons chopped walnuts

Cook the sweet potato and lemon juice in a large saucepan of boiling water for 15 minutes, or until tender. Drain and pat dry with paper towel. Allow to cool for 5 minutes.

Blend the sweet potato and 30 g (1 oz) of the butter in a food processor until smooth. Add the parmesan, chives and half the egg. Season and set aside to cool.

Brush a little of the egg mixture around the edges of half the won ton wrappers. Put 2 teaspoons of the mixture in the centre of half the won ton wrappers. Cover with the remaining wrappers and press the edges firmly together. Using a 7 cm (2¾ inch) cutter, cut the ravioli into circles.

Melt the remaining butter in a small saucepan over low heat and cook until golden brown.

Meanwhile, cook the pasta in a large saucepan of boiling salted water until *al dente*. Remove with a slotted spoon and drain well. Serve immediately, drizzled with the butter and sprinkled with the sage and walnuts.

SERVES 4

Tortellini with speck, asparagus and tomato

200 g (7 oz) piece speck (skin removed), roughly chopped
4 tomatoes
310 g (11 oz) asparagus, cut into 3 cm (1¼ inch) lengths
500 g (1 lb 2 oz) cheese tortellini
1 tablespoon olive oil
1 red onion, thinly sliced
1 tablespoon tomato paste (concentrated purée)
125 ml (4 fl oz/½ cup) chicken stock
2 teaspoons thyme leaves

Put the speck in a food processor and pulse until chopped.

Score a cross in the base of the tomatoes. Put in a heatproof bowl and cover with boiling water. Leave for 30 seconds, then transfer to cold water and peel the skin away from the cross. Roughly chop.

Cook the asparagus in a large saucepan of boiling water for 2 minutes, or until just tender. Remove with a slotted spoon and refresh in cold water. Drain. Cook the pasta in the same boiling water and cook until *al dente*. Drain well and return to the pan to keep warm.

Meanwhile, heat the oil in a saucepan over medium heat. Add the speck and onion and cook, stirring, for 2–3 minutes, or until the onion is soft. Add the tomato, tomato paste, stock and thyme and season. Cook, stirring, for 5 minutes. Add the pasta and asparagus to the tomato mixture and stir over low heat until warmed through.

SERVES 4–6

Agnolotti with creamy semi-dried tomato sauce and bacon

4 bacon slices
625 g (1 lb 6 oz) veal or chicken agnolotti
1 tablespoon olive oil
2 garlic cloves, finely chopped
110 g (3¾ oz/⅔ cup) thinly sliced semi-dried (sun-blushed) tomatoes
1 tablespoon chopped thyme
375 ml (13 fl oz/1½ cups) pouring (whipping) cream
1 teaspoon finely grated lemon zest
35 g (1¼ oz/⅓ cup) finely grated parmesan cheese

Grill (broil) the bacon for 5 minutes on each side, or until crisp and golden. Remove, drain well on paper towel, then break into pieces.

Cook the pasta in a large saucepan of boiling salted water until *al dente*. Drain well and return to the pan to keep warm.

Heat the oil in a frying pan over medium heat. Cook the garlic for 1 minute, or until just golden. Add the tomato and thyme and cook for a further 1 minute.

Add the cream, bring to the boil, then reduce the heat and simmer for about 6–8 minutes, or until the cream has thickened and reduced by one-third. Season and add the lemon zest and 2 tablespoons of the parmesan. Pour the sauce over the pasta. Sprinkle with the remaining parmesan and the bacon pieces.

SERVES 4

long

Chilli linguine with chermoula chicken

600 g (1 lb 5 oz) chicken breast fillets
500 g (1 lb 2 oz) chilli linguine

Chermoula
100 g (3½ oz) coriander (cilantro) leaves, chopped
60 g (2¼ oz) flat-leaf (Italian) parsley leaves, chopped
4 garlic cloves, crushed
2 teaspoons ground cumin
2 teaspoons ground paprika
125 ml (4 fl oz/½ cup) lemon juice
2 teaspoons lemon zest
100 ml (3½ fl oz) olive oil

Heat a large non-stick frying pan over medium heat. Add the chicken breasts and cook until tender. Remove from the pan and leave for 5 minutes before cutting into thin slices.

Cook the pasta in a large saucepan of boiling salted water until *al dente*. Drain well and return to the pan to keep warm.

Meanwhile, combine the chermoula ingredients in a bowl and add the sliced chicken. Serve the pasta topped with the chermoula chicken.

SERVES 4

Spaghettini with anchovies, capers and chilli

400 g (14 oz) spaghettini
125 ml (4 fl oz/½ cup) olive oil
4 garlic cloves, finely chopped
10 anchovy fillets, chopped
1 tablespoon baby capers, rinsed and squeezed dry
1 teaspoon chilli flakes
2 tablespoons lemon juice
2 teaspoons finely grated lemon zest
3 tablespoons chopped flat-leaf (Italian) parsley
3 tablespoons chopped basil leaves
3 tablespoons chopped mint
50 g (1¾ oz/½ cup) coarsely grated parmesan cheese,
    plus extra, to serve
extra virgin olive oil, to drizzle

Cook the pasta in a large saucepan of boiling salted water until *al dente*. Drain well and return to the pan to keep warm.

Heat the oil in a frying pan over medium heat. Cook the garlic for 2–3 minutes, or until starting to brown. Add the anchovies, capers and chilli and cook for 1 minute.

Add the pasta to the pan with the lemon juice, zest, parsley, basil, mint and parmesan. Season and toss together.

To serve, drizzle with a little extra oil and sprinkle with the parmesan.

SERVES 4

Tagliatelle with beef ragù

100 g (3½ oz) streaky bacon or pancetta (not trimmed),
    finely chopped
1 onion, finely chopped
3 garlic cloves, crushed
1 bay leaf
800 g (1 lb 12 oz) lean minced (ground) beef
500 ml (17 fl oz/2 cups) red wine
90 g (3¼ oz/⅓ cup) tomato paste (concentrated purée)
400 g (14 oz) tagliatelle
freshly grated parmesan cheese, to serve

Heat a large deep frying pan over medium–high heat. Add the bacon or pancetta and cook for 2 minutes, or until soft and just starting to brown. Add the onion, garlic and bay leaf and cook for 2 minutes, or until the onion is soft and just starting to brown.

Add the beef and stir for about 4 minutes or until the beef browns, breaking up any lumps with the back of a wooden spoon. Add the wine, tomato paste and 250 ml (9 fl oz/1 cup) water and stir well. Bring to the boil, then reduce the heat and simmer, covered, for 40 minutes. Remove the lid and cook for a further 40 minutes, or until reduced to a thick sauce.

Meanwhile, cook the pasta in a large saucepan of boiling salted water until *al dente*. Drain well and return to the pan to keep warm.

Serve the sauce over the pasta and top with grated parmesan.

SERVES 4

Spaghetti vongole

1 kg (2 lb 4 oz) baby clams (vongole)
375 g (13 oz) spaghetti
125 ml (4 fl oz/½ cup) extra virgin olive oil
40 g (1½ oz) butter
1 small onion, very finely chopped
6 large garlic cloves, finely chopped
125 ml (4 fl oz/½ cup) dry white wine
1 small red chilli, seeded and finely chopped
15 g (½ oz) chopped flat-leaf (Italian) parsley

Scrub the clams with a small stiff brush to remove any grit, discarding any that are open or cracked. Soak and rinse the clams in several changes of water over 1 hour, or until the water is clean and free of grit. Drain and set aside.

Cook the pasta in a large saucepan of boiling salted water until *al dente*. Drain well and return to the pan to keep warm.

Heat the oil and 1 tablespoon of the butter in a large saucepan over medium heat. Add the onion and half the garlic and cook for 10 minutes, or until lightly golden. Add the wine and cook for 2 minutes. Add the clams, chilli and the remaining butter and garlic. Cook, covered, for 8 minutes, shaking regularly, until the clams pop open. Discard any that are still closed.

Stir in the parsley and season. Add the pasta and toss together.

SERVES 4

Pasta alla Norma

185 ml (6 fl oz/¾ cup) olive oil
1 onion, finely chopped
2 garlic cloves, finely chopped
800 g (1 lb 12 oz) tinned chopped tomatoes
400 g (14 oz) bucatini
1 large eggplant (aubergine), about 500 g (1 lb 2 oz)
30 g (1 oz) basil leaves, torn, plus extra, to garnish
60 g (2¼ oz/½ cup) ricotta salata (see Note), crumbled
45 g (1½ oz/½ cup) grated pecorino or parmesan cheese
1 tablespoon extra virgin olive oil, to drizzle

Heat 2 tablespoons of the oil in a frying pan over medium heat. Cook the onion for 5 minutes. Stir in the garlic and cook for 30 seconds. Add the tomato and season. Reduce the heat to low and cook for 20–25 minutes, or until thick.

Cook the pasta in a large saucepan of boiling salted water until *al dente*. Drain well and return to the pan to keep warm.

Meanwhile, cut the eggplant lengthways into 5 mm (¼ inch) thick slices. Heat the remaining olive oil in a large frying pan over medium heat. Add the eggplant slices a few at a time and cook for 3–5 minutes, or until lightly browned on both sides. Remove from the pan and drain on crumpled paper towel.

Add the eggplant to the sauce with the basil, stirring over very low heat. Add the pasta to the sauce with half each of the ricotta and pecorino and toss together. Serve sprinkled with the remaining cheeses and basil and drizzle with oil.

SERVES 4–6

NOTE: Ricotta salata is a lightly salted, pressed ricotta cheese. If unavailable, use a mild feta cheese.

Creamy tomato and prawn tagliatelle

400 g (14 oz) dried egg tagliatelle
1 tablespoon olive oil
3 garlic cloves, finely chopped
20 medium raw prawns (shrimp), peeled and deveined,
    with tails intact
550 g (1 lb 4 oz) roma (plum) tomatoes, diced
2 tablespoons thinly sliced basil
125 ml (4 fl oz/½ cup) white wine
4 tablespoons pouring (whipping) cream
basil leaves, to garnish

Cook the pasta in a large saucepan of boiling salted water until *al dente*. Drain well, reserving 2 tablespoons of the cooking water. Return the pasta to the pan to keep warm.

Heat the oil and garlic in a large frying pan over low heat for 1–2 minutes. Increase the heat to medium, add the prawns and cook for 3–5 minutes, stirring frequently until cooked. Remove the prawns and keep warm.

Add the tomato and sliced basil and stir for 3 minutes, or until the tomato is soft. Pour in the wine and cream, bring to the boil and simmer for 2 minutes.

Purée the sauce in a blender. Return to the pan, then add the reserved pasta water and bring to a simmer. Stir in the prawns until heated through. Toss through the pasta and serve garnished with the basil leaves.

SERVES 4

Bavette with chicken, pine nuts and lemon

1.3 kg (3 lb) chicken
1 garlic bulb, cloves separated
and left unpeeled
3 tablespoons olive oil
30 g (1 oz) butter, softened
1 tablespoon finely chopped
thyme
125 ml (4 fl oz/½ cup) lemon
juice

500 g (1 lb 2 oz) bavette or
spaghetti
2 tablespoons currants
1 teaspoon finely grated lemon
zest
50 g (1¾ oz/⅓ cup) pine nuts,
toasted
15 g (½ oz) finely chopped
flat-leaf (Italian) parsley

Preheat the oven to 200°C (400°F/Gas 6). Remove the neck from the inside of the chicken and place the neck in a roasting tin. Rinse the inside of the chicken with cold water. Insert the garlic cloves into the cavity, then put the chicken in the tin.

Combine the oil, butter, thyme and lemon juice, then rub over the chicken. Season. Roast for 1 hour, or until the skin is golden and the juices run clear when the thigh is pierced with a skewer. Transfer the chicken to a bowl. Remove the garlic from the cavity, cool, then squeeze the garlic cloves out of their skins and finely chop.

Cook the pasta in a large saucepan of boiling salted water until *al dente*. Drain well and return to the pan to keep warm.

Meanwhile, pour the juices from the roasting tin into a saucepan and discard the neck. Add the currants, zest and chopped garlic, then simmer over low heat. Remove all the meat from the chicken and shred. Add the resting juices to the pan. Add the chicken, pine nuts, parsley and sauce to the pasta and toss.

SERVES 4–6

Fettucine with creamy spinach and roast tomato

6 roma (plum) tomatoes
40 g (1½ oz) butter
2 garlic cloves, crushed
1 onion, chopped
500 g (1 lb 2 oz) English spinach, trimmed
250 ml (9 fl oz/1 cup) vegetable stock
125 ml (4 fl oz/½ cup) thick (double/heavy) cream
500 g (1 lb 2 oz) fresh spinach fettucine
50 g (1¾ oz) shaved parmesan cheese

Preheat the oven to 220°C (425°F/ Gas 7). Cut the tomatoes in half lengthways, then cut each half into three wedges. Place the wedges on a lightly greased baking tray and roast for 30–35 minutes, or until softened and slightly golden.

Meanwhile, heat the butter in a large frying pan over medium heat. Add the garlic and onion and cook for 5 minutes, or until the onion is soft. Add the spinach, stock and cream. Increase the heat to high and bring to the boil. Simmer for 5 minutes. Remove from the heat and season. Set aside to cool slightly.

Meanwhile, cook the pasta in a large saucepan of boiling salted water until al dente. Drain well and return to the pan to keep warm.

Process the spinach mixture in a food processor until smooth. Toss through the pasta until well coated. Top with the roasted tomatoes and parmesan.

SERVES 4–6

Spaghettini with squid in black ink

1 kg (2 lb 4 oz) squid
2 tablespoons olive oil
1 onion, finely chopped
6 garlic cloves, finely chopped
1 bay leaf
1 small red chilli, seeded and
  thinly sliced
4 tablespoons white wine
4 tablespoons dry vermouth
250 ml (9 fl oz/1 cup) fish stock

60 g (2¼ oz/¼ cup) tomato
  paste (concentrated purée)
500 ml (17 fl oz/2 cups) tomato
  passata (puréed tomatoes)
15 g (½ oz) squid ink
500 g (1 lb 2 oz) spaghettini
½ teaspoon Pernod (optional)
4 tablespoons chopped flat-leaf
  (Italian) parsley
1 garlic clove, extra, crushed

To clean the squid, gently pull the tentacles away from the tube. Remove the intestines from the tentacles by cutting under the eyes, then remove the beak if it remains in the centre of the tentacles by using your fingers to push up the centre. Pull away the quill from inside the body and remove. Remove and discard any white membrane. Pull away the skin from the hood. Slice the squid into rings.

Heat the oil in a saucepan over medium heat. Add the onion and cook until golden. Add the garlic, bay leaf and chilli and cook for 2 minutes. Stir in the wine, vermouth, stock, tomato paste, passata and 250 ml (9 fl oz/1 cup) water. Increase the heat to high and bring to the boil. Reduce to a simmer. Cook for 45 minutes, or until the liquid has reduced by half. Add the squid ink and cook for 2 minutes.

Meanwhile, cook the pasta in a large saucepan of boiling salted water until *al dente*. Drain and return to the pan. Add the squid rings and Pernod. Cook for 4 minutes, or until cooked through. Stir in the parsley and the extra garlic and season.

SERVES 4–6

Summer seafood marinara

300 g (10½ oz) fresh saffron angel hair pasta
1 tablespoon extra virgin olive oil
30 g (1 oz) butter
2 garlic cloves, finely chopped
1 large onion, finely chopped
1 small red chilli, finely chopped
600 g (1 lb 5 oz) tinned peeled tomatoes, chopped
250 ml (9 fl oz/1 cup) white wine
zest of 1 lemon
½ tablespoon sugar
200 g (7 oz) scallops without roe
500 g (1 lb 2 oz) raw prawns (shrimp), peeled and deveined
300 g (10½ oz) clams (vongole)

Cook the pasta in a large saucepan of boiling salted water until *al dente*. Drain well and return to the pan to keep warm.

Heat the oil and butter in a large frying pan over medium heat. Add the garlic, onion and chilli and cook for 5 minutes, or until soft. Add the tomatoes and wine and bring to the boil. Cook for 10 minutes, or until the sauce has reduced and thickened slightly.

Add the lemon zest, sugar, scallops, prawns and clams. Cook, covered, for 5 minutes, or until the seafood is tender. Discard any clams that do not open. Season and serve the pasta topped with the sauce.

SERVES 4

Spicy eggplant
spaghetti

300 g (10½ oz) spaghetti
125 ml (4 fl oz/½ cup) extra virgin olive oil
2 red chillies, finely sliced
1 onion, finely chopped
3 garlic cloves, crushed
4 bacon slices, chopped
400 g (14 oz) eggplant (aubergine), diced
2 tablespoons balsamic vinegar
2 tomatoes, chopped
3 tablespoons shredded basil

Cook the pasta in a large saucepan of boiling salted water until *al dente*. Drain well and return to the pan to keep warm.

Heat 1 tablespoon of the oil in a large, deep frying pan over medium heat. Cook the chilli, onion, garlic and bacon for 5 minutes, or until the onion is golden and the bacon browned. Remove from the pan and set aside.

Add half the remaining oil to the pan and cook half the eggplant over high heat, tossing to brown on all sides. Remove and repeat with the remaining oil and eggplant. Return the bacon mixture and all the eggplant to the pan, add the vinegar, tomato and basil and cook until heated through. Season.

Serve the spaghetti topped with the eggplant mixture.

SERVES 4

Pastitsio

2 tablespoons oil
4 garlic cloves, crushed
2 onions, chopped
1 kg (2 lb 4 oz) minced (ground) beef
1 kg (2 lb 4 oz) tinned peeled tomatoes, chopped
250 ml (9 fl oz/1 cup) dry red wine
250 ml (9 fl oz/1 cup) beef stock
1 bay leaf

1 teaspoon dried mixed herbs
350 g (12 oz) ziti
3 eggs, lightly beaten
500 g (1 lb 2 oz) Greek-style yoghurt
200 g (7 oz) kefalotyri cheese, grated
½ teaspoon ground nutmeg
60 g (2¼ oz/½ cup) grated cheddar cheese
oakleaf lettuce, to serve

Heat the oil in a large heavy-based frying pan over medium heat. Cook the garlic and onion for 5 minutes, or until the onion is soft. Add the beef and cook over high heat until browned, then drain off any excess fat. Add the tomato, wine, stock, bay leaf and herbs and bring to the boil. Reduce the heat and simmer for 40 minutes. Season well.

Preheat the oven to 180°C (350°F/Gas 4). Meanwhile, cook the pasta in a large saucepan of boiling salted water until *al dente*. Drain well and spread in the base of a large ovenproof dish. Pour in half the egg and top with the sauce.

Combine the yoghurt, remaining egg, kefalotyri and nutmeg and pour over the top. Sprinkle with the cheddar and bake for 40 minutes, or until golden brown. Serve with oakleaf lettuce.

SERVES 6–8

Spaghetti puttanesca

400 g (14 oz) spaghetti
2 tablespoons olive oil
1 onion, finely chopped
2 garlic cloves, finely sliced
1 small red chilli, cored, seeded and sliced
6 anchovy fillets, finely chopped
400 g (14 oz) tinned chopped tomatoes
1 tablespoon fresh oregano, finely chopped
16 black olives, halved and pitted
2 tablespoons baby capers
1 handful basil leaves

Cook the pasta in a large saucepan of boiling salted water until *al dente*. Drain well and return to the pan to keep warm.

Heat the olive oil in a large saucepan over medium heat. Add the onion, garlic and chilli and cook for 8 minutes, or until the onion is soft. Add the anchovies and cook for a further 1 minute. Add the tomato, oregano, olive halves and capers and bring to the boil. Reduce the heat, season and simmer for 3 minutes.

Add the spaghetti to the sauce and toss together. Scatter the basil over the top.

SERVES 4

Spaghettini with asparagus and rocket

100 ml (3½ fl oz) extra virgin olive oil
16 thin asparagus spears, cut into 5 cm (2 inch) lengths
375 g (13 oz) spaghettini
120 g (4¼ oz) rocket, shredded
2 small red chillies, finely chopped
2 teaspoons finely grated lemon zest
1 garlic clove, finely chopped
100 g (3½ oz/1 cup) grated parmesan cheese
2 tablespoons lemon juice

Bring a large saucepan of water to the boil over medium heat. Add 1 tablespoon of the oil and a pinch of salt to the water and blanch the asparagus for 3–4 minutes. Remove the asparagus with a slotted spoon, refresh under cold water, drain and place in a bowl. Return the water to a rapid boil and add the spaghettini. Cook the pasta until *al dente*. Drain well and return to the pan to keep warm.

Meanwhile, add the rocket, chilli, lemon zest, garlic and 65 g (2¼ oz/⅔ cup) of the parmesan to the asparagus and mix well. Add to the pasta, pour on the lemon juice and remaining olive oil and season. Stir well to combine. Top with the remaining parmesan.

SERVES 4

Paprika veal with caraway fettuccine

3 tablespoons oil
1 kg (2 lb 4 oz) diced veal
  shoulder
1 large onion, thinly sliced
3 garlic cloves, finely chopped
60 g (2¼ oz/¼ cup) paprika

½ teaspoon caraway seeds
800 g (1 lb 12 oz) tinned
  chopped tomatoes, half
  drained
350 g (12 oz) fettuccine
40 g (1½ oz) butter, softened

Heat half the oil in a large saucepan over medium–high heat. Brown the veal in batches for 3 minutes per batch. Remove the veal from the pan and set aside with any pan juices.

Add the remaining oil to the pan and sauté the onion and garlic over medium heat for 5 minutes, or until softened. Add the paprika and ¼ teaspoon of the caraway seeds and stir for 30 seconds.

Add the chopped tomatoes and their liquid plus 125 ml (4 fl oz/½ cup) water. Return the veal to the pan with any juices, increase the heat to high and bring to the boil. Reduce the heat to low, then cover and simmer for 1 hour 15 minutes, or until the meat is tender and the sauce has thickened.

Meanwhile, cook the pasta in a large saucepan of boiling salted water until *al dente*. Drain well and return to the pan to keep warm.

Stir in the butter and the remaining caraway seeds. Serve immediately with the veal.

SERVES 4

Buckwheat pasta
with cabbage, potato and cheese sauce

350 g (12 oz) savoy cabbage,
  roughly chopped
175 g (6 oz) potatoes, cut into
  2 cm (¾ inch) cubes
500 g (1 lb 2 oz) buckwheat
  pasta (see Note)
4 tablespoons extra virgin
  olive oil

30 g (1 oz) sage, finely chopped
2 garlic cloves, finely chopped
350 g (12 oz) mixed cheeses
  (such as mascarpone, fontina,
  taleggio and gorgonzola)
grated parmesan cheese,
  to serve

Bring a large saucepan of salted water to the boil. Add the cabbage, potato and the pasta and cook for 3–5 minutes, or until the pasta is *al dente* and the vegetables are cooked. Drain well, reserving about 250 ml (9 fl oz/1 cup) of the cooking water.

Add the olive oil to the saucepan and gently cook the sage and garlic for about 1 minute. Add the mixed cheeses to the pan. Stir, then add the pasta, cabbage and potatoes. Season. Remove the saucepan from the heat and gently stir the mixture together, adding some of the reserved pasta water to loosen it up a little if necessary. Serve with parmesan.

SERVES 6

NOTE: Buckwheat pasta is called pizzoccheri in Italy. This type of pasta is popular in Valtellina, near the Swiss border, and is traditionally served with potatoes, cabbage and cheese.

Spaghetti Bolognese

60 g (2¼ oz) butter
1 onion, finely chopped
2 garlic cloves, crushed
1 celery stick, finely chopped
1 carrot, diced
50 g (1¾ oz) piece pancetta, diced
500 g (1 lb 2 oz) minced (ground) beef
1 tablespoon chopped oregano

250 ml (9 fl oz/1 cup) red wine
500 ml (17 fl oz/2 cups) beef stock
2 tablespoons tomato paste (concentrated purée)
800 g (1 lb 12 oz) tinned crushed tomatoes
400 g (14 oz) spaghetti
3 tablespoons grated parmesan cheese

Melt the butter in a large saucepan over medium heat. Add the onion and cook for 2–3 minutes, or until soft. Add the garlic, celery and carrot, and cook, stirring, over low heat, for 5 minutes. Increase the heat to high, add the pancetta, beef and oregano, and cook for 4–5 minutes or until browned.

Pour in the wine, reduce the heat and simmer for 4–5 minutes, or until absorbed. Add the stock, tomato paste and tomatoes and season. Cover with a lid and simmer for 1½ hours, stirring occasionally. Uncover and simmer for a further 1 hour, stirring occasionally.

Cook the pasta in a large saucepan of boiling salted water until *al dente*. Drain well and return to the pan to keep warm.

Top the pasta with the sauce. Serve with the parmesan.

SERVES 4

Ziti carbonara

1 tablespoon olive oil
200 g (7 oz) piece pancetta, cut into long thin strips
500 g (1 lb 2 oz) ziti
4 egg yolks
300 ml (10½ fl oz) pouring (whipping) cream
50 g (1¾ oz/½ cup) grated parmesan cheese, plus extra to serve
2 tablespoons finely chopped flat-leaf (Italian) parsley

Heat the olive oil in a non-stick frying pan over high heat. Cook the pancetta for 6 minutes, or until crisp and golden.

Meanwhile, cook the pasta in a large saucepan of boiling salted water until *al dente*. Drain well and return to the pan to keep warm.

Beat the egg yolks, cream and parmesan together in a bowl and season. Pour over the pasta in the saucepan and toss. Add the pancetta and parsley. Cook over very low heat for 30–60 seconds, or until the sauce has thickened and coats the pasta. Don't overheat or the eggs will scramble. Season and serve with extra parmesan.

SERVES 4–6

Tagliatelle with tuna, capers and rocket

3 garlic cloves, crushed
1 teaspoon finely grated lemon zest
4 tablespoons extra virgin olive oil
500 g (1 lb 2 oz) tuna, cut into 1.5 cm (⅝ inch) cubes
350 g (12 oz) fresh tagliatelle
200 g (7 oz) rocket (arugula) leaves, washed, dried
    and roughly chopped
4 tablespoons baby capers in salt, rinsed and squeezed dry
3 tablespoons lemon juice
2 tablespoons finely chopped flat-leaf (Italian) parsley

Combine the garlic, lemon zest and 1 tablespoon of the oil and the tuna in a bowl and season.

Meanwhile, cook the pasta in a large saucepan of boiling salted water until *al dente*. Drain well and return to the pan to keep warm.

Heat a non-stick frying pan over high heat. Sear the tuna for 30 seconds on each side. Add the rocket and capers and gently stir for 1 minute, or until the rocket has just wilted. Pour in the lemon juice and then remove from the heat.

Add the remaining oil, tuna mixture and parsley to the pasta. Season and toss.

SERVES 4

Creamy garlic prawn fettuccine

400 g (14 oz) fresh fettuccine
1 tablespoon olive oil
1 onion, finely chopped
3 garlic cloves, crushed
400 g (14 oz) tomatoes, seeded and chopped
3 tablespoons white wine
300 ml (10½ fl oz) pouring (whipping) cream
1 kg (2 lb 4 oz) raw prawns, peeled, deveined and
    tails intact
15 g (½ oz) roughly chopped basil

Cook the pasta in a large saucepan of boiling salted water until *al dente*. Drain well and return to the pan to keep warm.

Heat the oil in a large frying pan over medium–high heat. Cook the onion and garlic, stirring, for 4–5 minutes, or until the onion is soft. Add the tomato and wine and cook for 3 minutes, then add the cream. Bring to the boil, then reduce the heat to medium–low and simmer for 5 minutes, or until it slightly thickens.

Stir in the prawns, then simmer for 3–4 minutes, or until the prawns turn pink and are curled and cooked through. Toss with the pasta, stir in the basil and season.

SERVES 4

Spaghetti with meatballs

Meatballs

500 g (1 lb 2 oz) minced
   (ground) beef
40 g (1½ oz) fresh breadcrumbs
1 onion, finely chopped
2 garlic cloves, crushed
2 teaspoons worcestershire
   sauce
1 teaspoon dried oregano
30 g (1 oz/¼ cup) plain
   (all-purpose) flour
2 tablespoons olive oil

Sauce

800 g (1 lb 12 oz) tinned
   chopped tomatoes
1 tablespoon olive oil
1 onion, finely chopped
2 garlic cloves, crushed
2 tablespoons tomato paste
   (concentrated purée)
120 ml (4 fl oz) beef stock
2 teaspoons sugar

500 g (1 lb 2 oz) spaghetti
grated parmesan cheese, to serve

Combine the beef, breadcrumbs, onion, garlic, worcestershire sauce and oregano in a bowl and season. Mix well. Roll level tablespoons of the mixture into balls, dust with the flour and shake off the excess. Heat the oil in a frying pan over high heat. Cook the meatballs in batches, turning, until browned all over. Drain well.

Purée the tomatoes in a food processor. Heat the oil in a frying pan over medium heat. Add the onion and cook until soft. Add the garlic and cook for 1 minute. Add the puréed tomatoes, tomato paste, stock and sugar and stir to combine. Bring to the boil and add the meatballs. Reduce the heat and simmer for 15 minutes. Season.

Meanwhile, cook the pasta in a large saucepan of boiling salted water until *al dente*. Drain well and return to the pan to keep warm.

Top the pasta with the meatballs and sauce. Serve with parmesan.

SERVES 4

Spaghetti marinara

Tomato sauce
2 tablespoons olive oil
1 onion, finely chopped
1 carrot, finely chopped
2 garlic cloves, crushed
400 g (14 oz) tinned chopped
    tomatoes
125 ml (4 fl oz/½ cup) white
    wine
1 teaspoon sugar

3 tablespoons white wine
3 tablespoons fish stock
1 garlic clove, crushed

12 black mussels, cleaned
375 g (13 oz) spaghetti
30 g (1 oz) butter
125 g (4½ oz) squid, cleaned
    and cut into rings
125 g (4½ oz) skinless cod fillet,
    cut into bite-sized pieces
200 g (7 oz) prawns (shrimp),
    peeled and deveined
1 handful flat-leaf (Italian)
    parsley, chopped
200 g (7 oz) tinned clams,
    drained

Heat the oil in a saucepan over medium heat. Cook the onion and carrot for 10 minutes, or until browned. Add the garlic, tomato, wine and sugar. Bring to the boil, then reduce the heat and simmer for 30 minutes, stirring occasionally.

Heat the wine, stock and garlic in a large saucepan over high heat. Add the mussels. Cover and shake the pan for 5 minutes. Discard any unopened mussels and reserve the cooking liquid.

Cook the pasta in a large saucepan of boiling salted water until *al dente*. Drain well and return to the pan to keep warm.

Melt the butter in a frying pan over medium heat. Stir-fry the squid, cod and prawns in batches for 2 minutes, or until just cooked. Add to the tomato sauce along with the reserved cooking liquid, mussels, parsley and clams. Toss together.

SERVES 4

curly

Fusilli with roasted tomatoes, tapenade and bocconcini

800 g (1 lb 12 oz) cherry or teardrop tomatoes
   (or a mixture of both), halved if they are large
500 g (1 lb 2 oz) fusilli
300 g (10½ oz) baby bocconcini (fresh baby
   mozarella cheese), sliced
1 tablespoon chopped thyme

Tapenade
1½ tablespoons capers
2 small garlic cloves
185 g (6½ oz/1½ cups) sliced black olives
3 tablespoons lemon juice
4–5 tablespoons extra virgin olive oil

Preheat the oven to 200°C (400°F/ Gas 6). Place the tomatoes on a baking tray, season and roast for 10 minutes, or until slightly dried.

To make the tapenade, put the capers, garlic, olives and lemon juice in a food processor and mix together. With the motor running, gradually add the oil until the mixture forms a smooth paste.

Cook the pasta in a large saucepan of boiling salted water until *al dente*. Drain well and return to the pan to keep warm. Toss the tapenade and bocconcini through the pasta. Top with the tomatoes and thyme.

SERVES 4–6

Warm minted chicken and cotelli salad

250 g (9 oz) cotelli
125 ml (4 fl oz/½ cup) olive oil
1 large red capsicum (pepper)
3 boneless, skinless chicken
    breasts
6 spring onions (scallions), cut
    into 2 cm (¾ inch) lengths

4 garlic cloves, thinly sliced
35 g (1¼ oz) chopped mint
4 tablespoons cider vinegar
100 g (3½ oz) baby English
    spinach leaves

Cook the pasta in a large saucepan of boiling salted water until *al dente*. Drain well and return to the pan to keep warm. Stir in 1 tablespoon of the oil.

Meanwhile, cut the capsicum into quarters and remove the membrane and seeds. Cook, skin side up, under a hot grill (broiler) until the skin blackens and blisters. Cool in a plastic bag, then peel the skin. Cut into thin strips.

Put the chicken between two sheets of plastic wrap and press with the palm of your hand until slightly flattened.

Heat 1 tablespoon of the oil in a large frying pan over medium heat. Add the chicken and cook for 2–3 minutes each side, or until cooked through. Remove from the pan and cut into 5 mm (¼ inch) slices.

Add 1 tablespoon of the oil to the pan and add the spring onion, sliced garlic and capsicum. Cook, stirring, for 2–3 minutes, or until starting to soften. Add 25 g (1 oz) of the mint, the vinegar and the remaining oil and stir.

Combine the pasta, chicken, spinach, spring onion mixture and remaining mint. Toss together and season.

SERVES 4

Prosciutto and vegetable pasta bake

3 tablespoons olive oil
35 g (1¼ oz/⅓ cup) dry
  breadcrumbs
250 g (9 oz) mixed curly pasta,
  such as cotelli and fusilli
6 thin slices prosciutto, chopped
1 red onion, chopped
1 red capsicum (pepper), chopped

100 g (3½ oz) semi-dried
  (sun-blushed) tomatoes,
  chopped
3 tablespoons shredded basil
100 g (3½ oz/1 cup) grated
  parmesan cheese
4 eggs, lightly beaten
250 ml (9 fl oz/1 cup) milk

Preheat the oven to 180°C (350°F/ Gas 4). Lightly grease a 25 cm (10 inch) round ovenproof dish. Sprinkle the dish with 2 tablespoons of the breadcrumbs to coat the base and side.

Cook the pasta in a large saucepan of boiling water until al dente. Drain well and return to the pan to keep warm.

Heat 1 tablespoon of the oil in a large frying pan over medium heat. Add the prosciutto and onion and cook for 4–5 minutes, or until softened. Add the capsicum and semi-dried tomato and cook for a further 1–2 minutes. Add to t he pasta with the basil and parmesan and toss. Spoon into the prepared dish.

Place the eggs and milk in a bowl, whisk together, then season. Pour the egg mixture over the pasta. Season the remaining breadcrumbs, add the remaining oil and toss together. Sprinkle the seasoned breadcrumb mixture over the pasta. Bake for 40 minutes, or until set. Cut into wedges to serve.

SERVES 6–8

Cotelli with spring vegetables

500 g (1 lb 2 oz) cotelli
310 g (11 oz/2 cups) frozen peas
310 g (11 oz/2 cups) frozen broad beans, blanched and peeled
4 tablespoons olive oil
6 spring onions (scallions), cut into 3 cm (1¼ inch) pieces
2 garlic cloves, finely chopped
250 ml (9 fl oz/1 cup) chicken stock
12 thin fresh asparagus spears, cut into 5 cm (2 inch) lengths
1 lemon

Cook the pasta in a large saucepan of boiling salted water until *al dente*. Drain well and return to the pan to keep warm.

Meanwhile, cook the peas in a saucepan of boiling water for 1–2 minutes, until tender. Remove with a slotted spoon and plunge into cold water. Drain well. Add the broad beans to the saucepan, cook for 1–2 minutes, then drain and plunge into cold water. Remove and slip the skins off.

Heat 2 tablespoons of the olive oil in a frying pan over medium heat. Add the spring onion and garlic and cook for 2 minutes, or until softened. Pour in the stock and cook for 5 minutes, or until slightly reduced. Add the asparagus and cook for 3–4 minutes, or until bright green and just tender. Stir in the peas and broad beans and cook for 2–3 minutes, or until heated through.

Toss the remaining oil through the pasta. Add the vegetable mixture, ½ teaspoon finely grated lemon zest and 3 tablespoons lemon juice. Season and toss together.

SERVES 4

Fusilli salad with sherry vinaigrette

300 g (10½ oz) fusilli
250 g (9 oz/2 cups) cauliflower
125 ml (4 fl oz/½ cup) olive oil
16 slices pancetta
1 handful small sage leaves
100 g (3½ oz/⅔ cup) pine nuts,
   toasted
2 tablespoons finely chopped
   red Asian shallots

1½ tablespoons sherry vinegar
1 small red chilli, finely chopped
2 garlic cloves, crushed
1 teaspoon soft brown sugar
2 tablespoons orange juice
1 handful flat-leaf (Italian)
   parsley, finely chopped
35 g (1¼ oz/⅓ cup) shaved
   parmesan cheese

Cook the pasta in a large saucepan of boiling salted water until *al dente*. Drain and refresh under cold water. Drain well. Blanch the cauliflower florets in boiling water for 3 minutes, then drain and allow to cool.

Heat 1 tablespoon of olive oil in a non-stick frying pan over medium heat and cook the pancetta for 2 minutes, or until crisp. Drain on paper towel.

Add 1 tablespoon of oil and cook the sage leaves for 1 minute, or until crisp. Drain on paper towel. Combine the pasta, pine nuts and cauliflower in a bowl.

Heat the remaining olive oil. Add the shallots and cook gently for 2 minutes, or until soft. Remove from the heat then add the vinegar, chilli, garlic, brown sugar, orange juice and chopped parsley. Pour the warm dressing over the pasta and toss gently to combine.

Crumble the pancetta over the top and scatter with sage leaves and shaved parmesan. Serve warm.

SERVES 6

Cresti di gallo
with creamy tomato and bacon sauce

400 g (14 oz) cresti di gallo (see Note)
1 tablespoon olive oil
175 g (6 oz) bacon, thinly sliced
500 g (1 lb 2 oz) roma (plum) tomatoes, roughly chopped
125 ml (4 fl oz/½ cup) pouring (whipping) cream
2 tablespoons sun-dried tomato pesto
2 tablespoons finely chopped flat-leaf (Italian) parsley
50 g (1¾ oz/½ cup) finely grated parmesan cheese

Cook the pasta in a large saucepan of boiling salted water until *al dente*. Drain well and return to the pan to keep warm.

Meanwhile, heat the oil in a frying pan over high heat. Add the bacon and cook for 2 minutes, or until starting to brown. Reduce the heat to medium. Add the tomato and cook, stirring frequently, for 2 minutes, or until the tomato has softened but still holds its shape.

Add the cream and tomato pesto and stir until heated through. Remove from the heat. Add the parsley, then toss the sauce through the pasta with the parmesan.

SERVES 4

NOTE: Cresti di gallo pasta is named after the Italian word for 'cockscombs' because of its similarity to the crest of a rooster. You can also use cotelli or fusilli.

Fusilli with tuna, capers and parsley

425 g (15 oz) tinned tuna in springwater, drained
2 tablespoons olive oil
2 garlic cloves, finely chopped
2 small red chillies, finely chopped
3 tablespoons capers, rinsed and squeezed dry
15 g (¾ oz) chopped flat-leaf (Italian) parsley
3 tablespoons lemon juice
375 g (13 oz) fusilli
125 ml (4 fl oz/½ cup) chicken stock

Put the tuna in a bowl and flake lightly with a fork. Combine the oil, garlic, chilli, capers, parsley and lemon juice in a small bowl. Pour the mixture over the tuna and mix. Season.

Meanwhile, cook the pasta in a large saucepan of boiling salted water until *al dente*. Drain well and return to the pan to keep warm.

Toss the tuna mixture through the pasta, adding enough of the hot chicken stock to make it moist.

SERVES 4

Peppered pork, zucchini and garganelli

450 g (1 lb) pork fillet
3–4 teaspoons cracked black peppercorns
80 g (2¾ oz) butter
250 g (9 oz) garganelli
1 onion, halved and thinly sliced
2 large zucchini (courgette), thinly sliced
1 large handful fresh basil, torn
155 g (5½ oz/¾ cup) small black olives
60 g (2¼ oz/½ cup) grated romano cheese

Cut the pork fillet in half widthways and roll in the pepper and some salt. Heat half the butter in a large deep frying pan over medium heat. Add the pork and cook for 4 minutes on each side, or until golden brown and just cooked through. Remove from the pan and cut into 5 mm (¼ inch) slices, then set aside and keep warm.

Cook the pasta in a large saucepan of boiling salted water until *al dente*. Drain well and return to the pan to keep warm.

Meanwhile, melt the remaining butter in the frying pan over medium heat. Add the onion and cook, stirring, for about 3 minutes, or until soft. Add the zucchini and toss for 5 minutes, or until starting to soften. Add the basil, olives, sliced pork and any juices and toss well. Stir the pork mixture through the pasta, then season. Serve topped with the romano cheese.

SERVES 4

Cotelli, tomato and artichoke grill

350 g (12 oz) cotelli
285 g (10 oz) jar marinated artichoke hearts,
   drained and chopped
2 tablespoons olive oil
250 ml (9 fl oz/1 cup) pouring (whipping) cream
2 tablespoons chopped thyme
2 garlic cloves, crushed
75 g (2½ oz/¾ cup) grated parmesan cheese
210 g (7½ oz/1⅔ cups) grated cheddar cheese
950 g (2 lb 2 oz) tomatoes, cut into 5 mm (¼ inch) slices

Cook the pasta in a large saucepan of boiling salted water until al dente. Drain well and return to the pan to keep warm.

Lightly grease a 23 x 30 cm (9 x 12 inch) rectangular ovenproof dish. Stir the artichokes, olive oil, cream, thyme, garlic, half the parmesan and 155 g (5½ oz/ 1¼ cups) of the cheddar through the pasta and season. Spread evenly in the dish.

Arrange the tomatoes over the top, overlapping one another. Season, then sprinkle with the remaining cheese. Cook under a hot grill (broiler) for 6 minutes, or until the cheeses melt and are golden brown.

SERVES 4

Fusilli with chicken, mushroom and tarragon

375 g (13 oz) fusilli
2 tablespoons olive oil
350 g (12 oz) chicken
   tenderloins, cut into 2 cm
   (¾ inch) pieces
20 g (¾ oz) butter
400 g (14 oz) Swiss brown or
   button mushrooms, sliced
2 garlic cloves, finely chopped
125 ml (4 fl oz/½ cup) dry white
   wine

185 ml (6 fl oz/¾ cup) pouring
   (whipping) cream
1 teaspoon finely grated lemon
   zest
2 tablespoons lemon juice
1 tablespoon chopped tarragon
2 tablespoons chopped flat-leaf
   (Italian) parsley
25 g (1 oz/¼ cup) grated
   parmesan cheese, plus extra,
   to serve

Cook the pasta in a large saucepan of boiling salted water until *al dente*. Drain well and return to the pan to keep warm.

Meanwhile, heat 1 tablespoon of the oil in a large frying pan over high heat. Add the chicken and cook for 3–4 minutes, or until lightly browned. Remove from the pan.

Heat the butter and the remaining oil in the frying pan over high heat. Add the mushrooms and cook for 3 minutes. Add the garlic and cook for a further 2 minutes.

Pour in the wine, then reduce the heat to low and simmer for 5 minutes. Add the cream and chicken and simmer for about 5 minutes, or until thickened. Stir in the lemon zest, lemon juice, tarragon, parsley and parmesan. Season, then add the pasta, tossing until well combined. Serve with the extra parmesan.

SERVES 4

Fusilli with broccolini, chilli and olives

3 tablespoons olive oil
1 onion, finely chopped
3 garlic cloves
1 teaspoon chilli flakes
700 g (1 lb 9 oz) broccolini, cut into 1 cm (½ inch) pieces
125 ml (4 fl oz/½ cup) vegetable stock
400 g (14 oz) fusilli
90 g (3¼ oz/½ cup) black olives, pitted and chopped
1 handful flat-leaf (Italian) parsley, finely chopped
25 g (1 oz/¼ cup) grated pecorino cheese
2 tablespoons basil leaves, shredded

Heat the olive oil in a large non-stick frying pan over medium heat. Cook the onion, garlic and chilli until softened. Add the broccolini and cook for 5 minutes. Pour in the stock and cook, covered, for 5 minutes.

Meanwhile, cook the pasta in a large saucepan of boiling salted water until *al dente*. Drain well and return to the pan to keep warm.

When the broccolini is tender, remove from the heat. Add to the pasta with the olives, parsley, pecorino and basil, and season. Toss together to combine.

SERVES 4

Goulash with fusilli

400 g (14 oz) fusilli
2 tablespoons olive oil
1 large onion, sliced into thin wedges
600 g (1 lb 5 oz) rump steak, trimmed and cut into
    2 cm (¾ inch) cubes
1 tablespoon plain (all-purpose) flour
1 small green capsicum (pepper), diced
850 g (1 lb 14 oz) tinned diced tomatoes
1 teaspoon hot paprika
80 g (2¾ oz/⅓ cup) light sour cream

Cook the pasta in a large saucepan of boiling salted water until *al dente*. Drain well and return to the pan to keep warm.

Meanwhile, heat 1 tablespoon of the olive oil in a large frying pan over medium heat. Add the onion and cook, stirring, for 4–5 minutes, or until softened and golden. Remove the onion from the pan.

Heat the remaining olive oil in the same frying pan over high heat. Toss the steak cubes in the flour, shaking off any excess, then add to the pan and cook for 2 minutes to brown on all sides. Add the capsicum, tomato, paprika and the cooked onion and stir to combine.

Bring the mixture to the boil, then reduce the heat and simmer for 8–10 minutes, stirring occasionally. Season. To serve, spoon the goulash mixture over the pasta and top with sour cream.

SERVES 4

Sweet potato, rocket and walnut pasta salad

800 g (1 lb 12 oz) orange sweet potato, cut into
  2 cm (¾ inch) cubes
150 ml (5 fl oz) olive oil
125 g (4½ oz/1 cup) walnut pieces
350 g (12 oz) fricelli
150 g (5½ oz) white castello cheese (or other creamy
  soft-rind cheese), softened
2 garlic cloves, crushed
2 teaspoons lemon juice
½ teaspoon sugar
100 g (3½ oz) baby rocket (arugula)

Preheat the oven to 200°C (400°F/ Gas 6). Toss the orange sweet potato in
2 tablespoons of the oil and place in a single layer on a baking tray lined with
baking paper. Season. Roast, turning halfway through, for 30 minutes, or until
golden and cooked through.

Spread the walnuts on a baking tray and roast for 10 minutes, or until crisp.

Meanwhile, cook the pasta in a large saucepan of boiling salted water until
al dente. Drain well and return to the pan to keep warm.

Remove the rind from one-third of the cheese and cut the rest into cubes. Finely
chop 2 tablespoons of the walnuts. Combine with the garlic, lemon juice, sugar,
remaining oil and rindless cheese. Season. Combine the pasta, sweet potato,
rocket, cubed cheese and remaining walnuts in a bowl. Drizzle with the dressing
and toss together. Season.

SERVES 4

Chicken, broccoli and pasta bake

300 g (10½ oz) fusilli
425 g (15 oz) tinned cream of mushroom soup
2 eggs
185 g (6½ oz/¾ cup) whole-egg mayonnaise
1 tablespoon dijon mustard
210 g (7½ oz/1⅔ cups) grated cheddar cheese
600 g (1 lb 5 oz) chicken breast fillets, thinly sliced
400 g (14 oz) frozen broccoli pieces, thawed
40 g (1½ oz/½ cup) fresh breadcrumbs

Preheat the oven to 180°C (350°F/Gas 4). Cook the pasta in a large saucepan of boiling salted water until *al dente*. Drain well and return to the pan to keep warm.

Combine the soup, eggs, mayonnaise, mustard and half the cheese in a bowl.

Heat a lightly greased non-stick frying pan over medium heat. Add the chicken pieces and cook for 5–6 minutes, or until cooked through. Season, then set aside to cool.

Add the chicken and broccoli to the pasta. Pour the soup mixture over the top and stir until well combined. Transfer the mixture to a 3 litre (105 fl oz/12 cup) ovenproof dish. Sprinkle with the combined breadcrumbs and remaining cheese. Bake for 20 minutes, or until the top is golden brown.

SERVES 4

flat

Fresh vegetable lasagne with rocket

Balsamic syrup
4 tablespoons balsamic vinegar
1½ tablespoons brown sugar

16 asparagus spears, trimmed
and cut into 5 cm (2 inch)
lengths
150 g (5½ oz/1 cup) peas
2 large zucchini (courgettes),
cut into thin ribbons

2 fresh lasagne sheets
100 g (3½ oz) rocket (arugula)
leaves
1 large handful basil, torn
2 tablespoons olive oil
250 g (9 oz) ricotta cheese
150 g (5½ oz) semi-dried
tomatoes
shaved parmesan cheese,
to serve

Stir the vinegar and brown sugar in a saucepan over medium heat until the sugar dissolves. Reduce the heat and simmer for 3–4 minutes. Remove from the heat.

Bring a saucepan of salted water to the boil. Blanch the asparagus, peas and zucchini in separate batches until just tender. Remove and refresh each batch in cold water. Drain well. Return the cooking liquid to the boil. Cook the lasagne sheets in the water for 1–2 minutes, or until *al dente*. Drain. Cut each sheet in half lengthways.

Toss the vegetables and the rocket with the basil and olive oil. Season. Place one strip of pasta on a plate — one-third on the centre of the plate and two-thirds overhanging one side. Place some salad on the centre one-third, topped with some ricotta and tomato. Season and fold over one-third of the lasagne sheet. Top with another layer of salad, ricotta and tomato. Fold back the final layer of pasta and garnish with salad and tomato. Repeat with the remaining pasta, salad, ricotta and tomato. Drizzle with the balsamic syrup and serve with the parmesan.

SERVES 4

Roast pumpkin
sauce on pappardelle

1.4 kg (3 lb 2 oz) butternut pumpkin (squash),
  cut into 2 cm (¾ inch) pieces
4 garlic cloves, crushed
3 teaspoons thyme leaves, plus extra to serve
100 ml (3½ fl oz) olive oil
500 g (1 lb 2 oz) pappardelle
2 tablespoons whipping (pouring) cream
185 ml (6 fl oz/¾ cup) hot chicken stock
30 g (1 oz) shaved parmesan cheese

Preheat the oven to 200°C (400°F/Gas 6). Combine the pumpkin, garlic, thyme and 3 tablespoons of the olive oil in a bowl and toss together. Season.

Transfer to a baking tray and cook for 30 minutes, or until tender and golden.

Meanwhile, cook the pasta in a large saucepan of boiling salted water until *al dente*. Drain well and return to the pan to keep warm. Toss through the remaining oil and keep warm.

Place the pumpkin and the cream in a food processor or blender and process until smooth. Add the hot stock and process until smooth and combined. Season and gently toss through the pasta. Sprinkle with parmesan and extra thyme, if desired.

SERVES 4

Lasagnette with spicy chicken meatballs

750 g (1 lb 10 oz) minced (ground) chicken
2 tablespoons chopped coriander (cilantro) leaves
1½ tablespoons red curry paste
2 tablespoons oil
1 red onion, finely chopped
3 garlic cloves, crushed
875 g (1 lb 15 oz/3½ cups) ready-made tomato pasta sauce
2 teaspoons soft brown sugar
350 g (12 oz) lasagnette

Line a tray with baking paper. Combine the meat, coriander and 1 tablespoon of the curry paste. Roll heaped tablespoons of the mixture into balls and put on the tray. Refrigerate.

Heat the oil in a large deep frying pan over medium heat. Cook the onion and garlic for 2–3 minutes, or until softened. Add the remaining curry paste and cook, stirring, for 1 minute, or until fragrant. Add the pasta sauce and sugar and stir well. Reduce the heat and add the meatballs. Cook, turning halfway through, for 10 minutes, or until the meatballs are cooked through.

Meanwhile, cook the pasta in a large saucepan of boiling salted water until *al dente*. Drain well and return to the pan to keep warm.

Serve topped with the sauce and meatballs. Garnish with coriander, if desired.

SERVES 4

Tuna and chermoula on pappardelle

500 g (1 lb 2 oz) sweet potato, cut into 2 cm (¾ inch) cubes
100 ml (3½ fl oz) olive oil
60 g (2¼ oz) coriander (cilantro) leaves, finely chopped
40 g (1½ oz) flat-leaf (Italian) parsley, chopped
3 garlic cloves, crushed
3 teaspoons ground cumin
3 tablespoons lemon juice
4 x 180 g (6 oz) tuna steaks
400 g (14 oz) pappardelle

Preheat the oven to 200°C (400°F/Gas 6). Toss the sweet potato in 2 tablespoons of the oil. Place on a baking tray and roast for 25–30 minutes, or until tender.

To make the chermoula, put the coriander, parsley, garlic, cumin and ¾ teaspoon cracked black pepper in a small food processor and process until a rough paste forms. Transfer to a bowl and stir in the lemon juice and 1 tablespoon of the oil.

Put the tuna in a non-metallic bowl, cover with 2 tablespoons of the chermoula and toss. Marinate in the fridge for 20 minutes.

Meanwhile, cook the pasta in a large saucepan of boiling salted water until *al dente*. Drain well and return to the pan to keep warm. Mix in the remaining chermoula and oil.

Heat a lightly oiled chargrill pan over high heat. Cook the tuna for 2 minutes on each side, or until done to your liking. Cut into 2 cm (¾ inch) cubes and toss through the pasta with the sweet potato.

SERVES 4

Stracci with artichokes and chargrilled chicken

1 tablespoon olive oil
3 boneless, skinless chicken breasts
500 g (1 lb 2 oz) stracci
8 slices prosciutto
280 g (10 oz) jar artichokes in oil, drained and
    quartered, oil reserved
150 g (5½ oz) semi-dried (sun-blushed) tomatoes,
    thinly sliced
80 g (2¾ oz) baby rocket (arugula)
2–3 tablespoons balsamic vinegar

Lightly brush a frying or chargrill pan with the oil and heat over high heat. Cook the chicken for 6–8 minutes each side, or until cooked through. Cut into thin slices on the diagonal.

Meanwhile, cook the pasta in a large saucepan of boiling salted water until *al dente*. Drain well and return to the pan to keep warm.

Put the prosciutto on a lined baking tray and cook under a hot grill (broiler) for 2 minutes each side, or until crisp. Cool slightly and break into pieces.

In a bowl, combine the pasta with the chicken, prosciutto, artichokes, tomato and rocket and toss. Whisk together 3 tablespoons of the reserved artichoke oil and the balsamic vinegar and toss through the pasta mixture. Season.

SERVES 6

Freeform ricotta and mushroom lasagne

250 g (9 oz/1 cup) ricotta cheese
65 g (2¼ oz/⅔ cup) grated
parmesan cheese
3½ tablespoons olive oil
1 onion, thinly sliced
2 garlic cloves, crushed
500 g (1 lb 2 oz) Swiss brown
mushrooms, sliced

300 ml (10½ fl oz) ready-made
tomato pasta sauce
6 sheets fresh lasagne, cut in
half, then cut into 12 cm
(4½ inch) squares
200 g (7 oz) baby English
spinach leaves, washed

Mix the ricotta with half the parmesan and season. Heat 2 tablespoons of oil in a large frying pan, add the onion and cook for 2 minutes, or until it softens. Add the garlic and mushrooms and cook for 1–2 minutes, or until the mushrooms start to soften. Add the tomato pasta sauce and cook for a further 5–6 minutes, or until the sauce starts to thicken. Season well.

Meanwhile, cook the pasta in a large saucepan of boiling salted water until *al dente*. Drain well and return to the pan to keep warm.

Put the spinach in a pan with just the water clinging to the leaves. Cover and cook over medium heat for 1–2 minutes, or until the spinach has wilted.

To assemble, place a pasta square on the base of each plate. Top with the mushroom sauce, then place another pasta square on top. Spread the ricotta mixture evenly over the surface, leaving a 2 cm (¾ inch) border. Top with the spinach. Place another pasta square on top, drizzle with oil, then sprinkle with the parmesan. Season.

SERVES 4

Creamy chicken and peppercorn pappardelle

2 boneless, skinless chicken breasts
30 g (1 oz) butter
1 onion, halved and thinly sliced
2 tablespoons drained green peppercorns, slightly crushed
125 ml (4 fl oz/½ cup) white wine
300 ml (10½ fl oz) pouring (whipping) cream
400 g (14 oz) fresh pappardelle
80 g (2¾ oz/⅓ cup) sour cream (optional)
2 tablespoons chopped chives

Cut the chicken in half so that you have four flat fillets and season. Melt the butter in a frying pan over medium heat. Add the chicken and cook for 3 minutes on each side, or until lightly browned and cooked through. Remove from the pan, cut into slices and keep warm.

Add the onion and peppercorns to the same pan and cook over medium heat for 3 minutes, or until the onion has softened slightly. Add the wine and cook for 1 minute, or until reduced by half. Stir in the cream and cook for 4–5 minutes, or until thickened slightly, then season.

Meanwhile, cook the pasta in a large saucepan of boiling salted water until *al dente*. Drain well and return to the pan to keep warm.

Mix together the pasta, chicken and any juices and cream sauce. Serve topped with sour cream and sprinkled with chives.

SERVES 4

Blue cheese and walnut lasagnette

375 g (13 oz) lasagnette
100 g (3½ oz/1 cup) walnuts
40 g (1½ oz) butter
3 French shallots, finely chopped
1 tablespoon brandy or cognac
250 ml (9 fl oz/1 cup) crème fraîche
200 g (7 oz) gorgonzola cheese, crumbled (see Note)
70 g (2½ oz) baby English spinach leaves

Preheat the oven to 200°C (400°F/Gas 6). Cook the pasta in a large saucepan of boiling salted water until *al dente*. Drain well and return to the pan to keep warm.

Meanwhile, put the walnuts on a baking tray and roast for 5 minutes, or until golden and toasted. Cool, then roughly chop.

Heat the butter in a large saucepan over medium heat. Add the shallots and cook for 1–2 minutes, or until soft. Add the brandy and simmer for 1 minute, then stir in the crème fraîche and gorgonzola. Cook for 3–4 minutes, or until the cheese has melted and the sauce has thickened.

Stir in the spinach and toasted walnuts, reserving 1 tablespoon for garnish. Heat gently until the spinach has just wilted. Season. Gently mix the sauce through the pasta. Serve sprinkled with the reserved walnuts.

SERVES 4

NOTE: The gorgonzola needs to be young as this gives a sweeter, milder flavour to the sauce.

Pappardelle with salmon and gremolata

30 g (1 oz) chopped flat-leaf (Italian) parsley
3 teaspoons grated lemon zest
2 garlic cloves, finely chopped
400 g (14 oz) pappardelle
3 tablespoons extra virgin olive oil
500 g (1 lb 2 oz) fresh salmon fillet
2 teaspoons olive oil, extra

To make the gremolata, put the parsley, lemon zest and garlic in a bowl and mix together well.

Cook the pasta in a large saucepan of boiling salted water until *al dente*. Drain well and return to the pan. Add the olive oil and toss gently. Add the gremolata to the pan with the pasta and toss.

Remove the skin and any bones from the salmon. Heat the extra olive oil in a frying pan over medium heat. Cook the salmon for 3–4 minutes, turning once during cooking. Take care not to overcook the fish. Flake the salmon into large pieces and toss through the pasta. Season.

SERVES 4

Freeform wild mushroom lasagne

10 g (¼ oz) dried porcini mushrooms
350 g (12 oz) mixed wild mushrooms (such as shiitake, oyster and Swiss brown)
30 g (1 oz) butter
1 small onion, halved and thinly sliced
1 tablespoon chopped thyme
3 egg yolks
125 ml (4 fl oz/½ cup) thick (double/heavy) cream
100 g (3½ oz/1 cup) grated parmesan cheese
8 fresh lasagne sheets (10 x 25 cm/4 x 10 inch)

Soak the porcini in 3 tablespoons boiling water for 15 minutes. Strain through a sieve, reserving the liquid. Cut the larger mushrooms in half.

Heat the butter in a frying pan over medium heat. Cook the onion for 2 minutes, or until just soft. Add the thyme, mushrooms and porcini and cook for about 1–2 minutes, or until softened. Add the reserved mushroom liquid and cook for 2 minutes, or until the liquid has evaporated. Set aside.

Beat the egg yolks, cream and half the parmesan in a large bowl. Cook the pasta in a large saucepan of boiling salted water until *al dente*. Drain well and toss gently in the egg mixture. Reheat the mushrooms.

To serve, place one sheet of folded lasagne on a plate. Top with some mushrooms, then another sheet of folded lasagne. Drizzle with any remaining egg mixture and sprinkle with the remaining parmesan.

SERVES 4

Roast duck with fresh pappardelle

250 g (9 oz) baby bok choy (pak choy), washed and
    leaves separated
600 g (1 lb 5 oz) fresh pappardelle
1 Chinese roast duck, skin removed (see Note)
4 tablespoons peanut oil
3 garlic cloves, crushed
3 teaspoons finely chopped fresh ginger
35 g (1¼ oz) chopped coriander (cilantro) leaves
2 tablespoons hoisin sauce
2 tablespoons oyster sauce

Bring a large saucepan of water to the boil and blanch the bok choy for
1–2 minutes, or until tender, but still crisp. Remove with a slotted spoon and
keep warm.

Meanwhile, cook the pasta in a large saucepan of boiling salted water until
al dente. Drain well and return to the pan to keep warm.

Remove the duck meat from the bones and finely shred. Heat the peanut oil in a
small saucepan over high heat and bring it up to smoking point. Remove from the
heat and allow to cool for 1 minute, then swirl in the garlic and ginger to infuse
the oil. Be careful not to allow the garlic to burn or it will turn bitter.

Pour the hot oil over the pasta and add the bok choy, duck, coriander, hoisin and
oyster sauces. Toss well, season and serve immediately.

SERVES 4–6

NOTE: Chinese roast duck can be bought from Asian speciality shops.

Smoked salmon
stracci in Champagne sauce

375 g (13 oz) fresh stracci (see Note)
1 tablespoon olive oil
2 large garlic cloves, crushed
125 ml (4 fl oz/½ cup) Champagne
250 ml (9 fl oz/1 cup) thick (double/heavy) cream
200 g (7 oz) smoked salmon, cut into thin strips
2 tablespoons small capers in brine, rinsed and patted dry
2 tablespoons chopped chives
2 tablespoons chopped dill

Cook the pasta in a large saucepan of boiling salted water until *al dente*. Drain well and return to the pan to keep warm.

Meanwhile, heat the oil in a large frying pan over medium heat. Cook the garlic for 30 seconds. Pour in the Champagne and cook for 2 minutes, or until the liquid is reduced slightly. Add the cream and cook for about 3–4 minutes, or until the sauce has thickened.

Add the sauce, salmon, capers and herbs to the pasta and toss gently. Season.

SERVES 4

NOTES: Stracci is sold fresh and dried — either is suitable for this recipe — or you can use fresh or dried fettucine or tagliatelle.

Seafood lasagne

1 tablespoon olive oil
30 g (1 oz) butter
1 onion, finely chopped
2 garlic cloves, crushed
400 g (14 oz) prawns (shrimp),
  peeled and deveined
500 g (1 lb 2 oz) firm white fish
  fillets, cut into small pieces
250 g (9 oz) scallops with roe
750 g (1 lb 10 oz) ready-made
  tomato pasta sauce
1 tablespoon tomato paste
  (concentrated purée)
1 teaspoon soft brown sugar

60 g (2¼ oz/½ cup) grated
  cheddar cheese
25 g (1 oz/¼ cup) grated
  parmesan cheese
250 g (9 oz) lasagne sheets

Cheese sauce

120 g (4¼ oz) butter
85 g (3 oz/⅔ cup) plain
  (all-purpose) flour
1.5 litres (52 fl oz/6 cups) milk
250 g (9 oz/2 cups) grated
  cheddar cheese
100 g (3½ oz/1 cup) grated
  parmesan cheese

Preheat the oven to 180°C (350°F/Gas 4). Grease a 2.5 litre (87 fl oz/10 cup) ovenproof dish. Heat the oil and butter in a saucepan. Add the onion and cook for 2–3 minutes. Add the garlic and cook for 30 seconds. Add the prawns and fish and cook for 2 minutes, then add the scallops. Cook for 1 minute. Stir in the pasta sauce, tomato paste and sugar and simmer for 5 minutes.

To make the sauce, melt the butter in a saucepan over low heat, then stir in the flour and cook for 1 minute. Stir in the milk. Simmer for 2 minutes, stirring, then mix in the cheddar and parmesan cheeses. Season. Line the dish with a layer of lasagne sheets. Spoon one-third of the seafood sauce into the dish. Top with one-third of the cheese sauce. Repeat until you have three layers, ending with a layer of cheese sauce. Sprinkle with the cheeses. Bake for 30 minutes, or until golden.

SERVES 6

Pappardelle with lamb shank, rosemary and red wine ragù

1½ tablespoons olive oil
1 large onion, finely chopped
1 large carrot, finely diced
2 celery stalks, finely diced
2 bay leaves
1.5 kg (3 lb 5 oz) lamb shanks
4 garlic cloves, finely chopped
1 tablespoon chopped rosemary
750 ml (26 fl oz/3 cups) dry red wine

1 litre (35 fl oz/4 cups) beef stock
500 ml (17 fl oz/2 cups) tomato passata (puréed tomatoes)
½ teaspoon finely grated lemon zest
500 g (1 lb 2 oz) pappardelle
flat-leaf (Italian) parsley leaves, to garnish

Heat 1 tablespoon of the oil in a large saucepan over medium heat. Add the onion, carrot, celery and bay leaves and cook, stirring often, for 10 minutes, or until the onion is lightly browned. Remove from the pan.

Heat some extra oil in the pan and cook the shanks in two batches, turning occasionally, for 15 minutes, or until browned. Remove from the pan. Add the garlic and rosemary to the pan. Cook for 30 seconds, or until golden. Return the vegetables to the pan, then stir in the wine, stock, passata, zest and 250 ml (9 fl oz/1 cup) water. Add the shanks and bring to the boil. Reduce the heat and simmer, uncovered, for 2¼ hours, or until the lamb is tender. Cook the pasta in a saucepan of boiling salted water until *al dente*. Drain well and return to the pan to keep warm. Remove the shanks from the sauce and remove the meat from the bones. Return the meat to the sauce and stir. Season. Toss the pasta through the sauce. Garnish with the parsley.

SERVES 6–8

Pumpkin, spinach and ricotta lasagne

3 tablespoons olive oil
1.5 kg (3 lb 5 oz) butternut
    pumpkin (squash), cut into
    1.5 cm (⅝ inch) dice
500 g (1 lb 2 oz) English spinach
    leaves
4 fresh lasagne sheets

500 g (1 lb 2 oz/2 cups) ricotta
    cheese
2 tablespoons pouring
    (whipping) cream
25 g (1 oz/¼ cup) grated
    parmesan cheese
pinch ground nutmeg

Heat the oil in a non-stick frying pan over medium heat. Add the pumpkin and cook, stirring occasionally, for 15 minutes, or until tender. Season and keep warm.

Cook the spinach in a large saucepan of boiling water for 30 seconds, or until wilted. Using a slotted spoon, transfer to a bowl of cold water. Drain well and squeeze out as much excess water as possible. Finely chop the spinach. Add the lasagne sheets to the saucepan of boiling water and cook, stirring occasionally, until *al dente*. Drain. Cut each sheet widthways into thirds.

Combine the ricotta, cream, parmesan, spinach and nutmeg in a small saucepan over low heat. Stir for 2–3 minutes, or until warmed through.

Place a piece of lasagne on the base of each plate. Using half the pumpkin, top each of the sheets, then cover with another piece of lasagne. Use half the ricotta mixture to spread over the lasagne sheets, then add another lasagne piece. Top with the remaining pumpkin, then remaining ricotta mixture. Season well and serve immediately.

SERVES 4

Pappardelle with salami, leek and provolone cheese

375 g (13 oz) pappardelle
2 tablespoons olive oil
2 leeks, thinly sliced (including some of the green section)
2 tablespoons white wine
800 g (1 lb 12 oz) tinned diced tomatoes
150 g (5½ oz) sliced mild salami, cut into strips
1 large handful basil leaves, torn
125 g (4½ oz) provolone cheese, cut into 3 cm
    (1¼ inch) wide strips
30 g (1 oz) grated parmesan cheese

Cook the pasta in a large saucepan of boiling salted water until *al dente*. Drain well and return to the pan to keep warm.

Meanwhile, heat the olive oil in a large deep frying pan over low heat. Add the leek and cook for 4 minutes, or until soft but not browned. Increase the heat to medium, add the wine and stir until almost evaporated.

Add the tomato and salami. Season and simmer for 5 minutes, or until reduced slightly. Toss the tomato sauce mixture, basil and provolone lightly through the pasta. Sprinkle with the parmesan.

SERVES 4

index